THE HARE NEVER LOST

A GUIDE TO PROSPERITY

GEET BATRA

ISBN: 978-93-341-4384-3

Cover design by: FREELANCER

This is my First book, and is dedicated to my father, Prem Kumar Batra (1946-2023). In my pursuit of the rat race, I failed to recognize his true prosperity. Now, I understand the richness he embodied.

"True prosperity isn't found in the chase but in the quiet wisdom of the journey. Listen to the whispers of your spirit guide and embrace the abundance within."

Preface

In the tapestry of life, there are moments that define our journey, guiding us toward our true path. For me, one such moment was the reconnection with my spirit guide, the Hare. After many years of searching and seeking, it was through this profound reconnection that I discovered the inspiration and insight to craft this book, "The Hare Never Lost – A Guide to Prosperity." Before diving into the rich lessons of this book, it's important to understand the symbolic difference between the Hare and the Rabbit. While both creatures are often confused for one another, the Hare stands out as a more fitting guide for my journey to prosperity. The Hare is known for its agility, speed, and independence. Unlike Rabbits, which tend to burrow and stay close to the ground, Hares live in open spaces, ready to leap into action. They represent adaptability, quick thinking, and boldness—traits essential for navigating life's opportunities and challenges with prosperity in mind. The Rabbit, on the other hand, tends to represent timidity, caution, and vulnerability. While Rabbits live in groups, relying on burrows for protection, Hares are solitary creatures, trusting in their instincts and resilience.

Hare says prosperity comes to those who are unafraid to leap into the unknown, embrace change, and run their own race. The Hare, with its gentle wisdom and boundless energy, became a beacon of clarity and creativity in my life. This guide, who had been quietly present yet unobtrusive, emerged as a profound influence, helping me navigate the intricate pathways to prosperity. It was through the Hare's guidance that I was able to explore the depths of shamanic journeys and incorporate these transformative experiences into the pages of this book. As you embark on this journey through the pages of "The Hare Never Lost," I hope you find inspiration and guidance, just as I did. May the wisdom of the Hare and the insights within these pages lead you to your own path of prosperity and fulfillment. With profound gratitude, Geet Batra
As you embark on this journey through the pages of "The Hare Never Lost," I hope you find inspiration and guidance, just as I did. May the wisdom of the Hare and the insights within these pages lead you to your own path of prosperity and fulfillment.

With profound gratitude,

Geet Batra

Acknowledgements

As I reflect on this journey, I am overwhelmed with gratitude for the people who have supported and inspired me along the way. My deepest thanks go to my teacher, Nithya Chellam, whose unwavering belief in my potential and encouragement to transcend limitations have been a cornerstone of my growth. Her dedication to nurturing my abundance has been instrumental in shaping the framework of this book.

I am also profoundly grateful to my dear friends, Priya Dhar and Aanchal Saraf. Their healing journeys and steadfast support have been a source of strength and rejuvenation. I have basked in the prosperity they helped me manifest, and their contributions have been invaluable. Additionally, I must extend heartfelt thanks to Natasha Bhasin Kukreja , whose gentle suggestion to connect with my animal spirit guide, the Hare, was the catalyst for this book. Her insight led me to engage with the Hare daily, igniting the creativity and speed that shaped this work.

My Journey with Access Consciousness in Last 5 Years prepared me; Now I am a Heal Your Life workshop Leader; I have been Following Louise Hay for last 16 years; But its only now that i could Receive from her Work contributing to me and I being a contribution to every Life i touch.

Special thanks to Louise Hay who had always been angel by my shoulder always; her work contributed to my understanding and growth in the field of prosperity, abundance, self-awareness and self-love. Your wisdom and guidance have inspired this book and its teachings.

Eternally Grateful for all of you!

Prologue

The Hare That Never Left (Even When I Tried to Ghost Him)

So, here's the deal: I have a spirit guide. He's a Hare. And for reasons I still can't quite explain, I've spent most of my life running away from him—ironic, right? A Hare and a human, both running, but only one of us knows why. (Spoiler: it's not me.)

It all started innocently enough. I completed not one but multiple Shamanic Practitioner courses, including the advanced ones, where you're supposed to "connect deeply" with your spirit guide and unlock the mysteries of the universe. But instead of fully embracing my mystical calling, I took the 'ghosting my spirit guide' approach. Why? No clue. It's like I signed up for a deep spiritual partnership and then left the Hare on read for years.

Yet, despite my epic dodging skills, the Hare never got the memo that I was...well, not ready for his wisdom. I'd sense him in meditations, see glimpses of him in dreams, and even spot random hare posts on social media when I was trying to avoid anything remotely spiritual. His message? "Hey, still here, still waiting for you to stop being a flight risk."

To his credit, my spirit guide has the patience of a saint and the agility of, well, a Hare. He's been my loyal companion, popping up when I least expect it (and let's be honest, least want it). If spirit guides could roll their eyes, I'm sure mine would be doing it constantly. But no, the Hare never judges. He just shows up—unconditionally loving, endlessly supportive, and silently exuding "I'll be right here when you stop running from your life's purpose."

I've tried everything to avoid the depth of this relationship. Meditation? Sure, but the second I felt his presence, I'd shift gears: "Oh wow, I suddenly have a deep urge to clean the entire house." I'd pick up my phone, only for a random post about hares to pop up on Instagram, and the Hare would be like, "Really? That's your plan? Distraction? Again?"

Even so, the Hare didn't push. His energy is fast and creative, but he's mastered the art of waiting. Every time I came up with a new excuse not to connect, he just sat there, calm and cool, like, "Take your time. I've got nothing but love, creativity, and wisdom waiting for you when you're ready."

And now, here we are—years of dodging later, and I'm finally sitting down to tell you the story of how I stopped running from my spirit guide. Turns out, the Hare was right all along (shocking, I know). This book is about what happens when you finally stop pretending you don't need the guidance of a wise, slightly smug, and incredibly persistent Hare in your life.

So here's to the Hare, who taught me that no matter how fast I run, he's faster. And maybe—just maybe—I should have stopped running a long time ago. But hey, at least now I have plenty of stories to share about how I ghosted my spirit guide, and how he patiently watched me sprint in circles, waiting for me to wise up and listen.

Freedom of Choice is your biggest power; Do not sell it for Approval.

I will speak louder if you don't hear my whispers; And I will still honor your choice to not listen

Chapter 1

The Spirit of Prosperity

It was a quiet evening, the kind where the world seemed to hold its breath. The gentle pitter-patter of rain in my ears as I sat on my chair, the sky shifting from the deep purples of twilight to the dark navy of night. I had been thinking of doing a shamanic journey for a long time.—a practice that always brought me guidance and clarity. Tonight, I sought answers about prosperity, a word that had been buzzing in my mind but one that felt elusive, like a shadow that never quite revealed its form.

I closed my eyes and focused on my breath, grounding myself, and feeling the earth beneath me. The rhythm of my breath slowed, and soon the world around me dissolved. I began to drift, moving deeper into the realms of my inner landscape, guided by an ancient pulse, one that connected me to the energies around and within me.

Without words, I knew why the hare had come. I had called for it with a question that had weighed heavily on my heart: What is prosperity?

The hare moved gracefully, leading me to a clearing bathed in soft, golden light. There, surrounded by fields of lush, green grass, flowers, and trees, the hare paused and turned to me. It sat back on its hind legs, its eyes meeting mine with an intensity that told me I was about to learn something deeply important.

In the stillness, I heard the hare's voice, though its mouth did not move. It spoke directly to my heart, the words echoing through my being.

"Prosperity," the hare began, "is often misunderstood as something that can be measured, something you can hold in your hands. Many believe it is simply the accumulation of money, of wealth, but that is only one small part of a much larger picture."

I felt myself nodding, knowing the truth in those words. Like many, I had often fallen into the trap of thinking prosperity was tied only to financial success. But deep down, I knew there was more.

"True prosperity," the hare continued, "is not about how much you have in the physical sense. It is about the abundance of love that fills your heart, the care you receive and give to others, the time you have to do what matters to you. It is about your health, your well-being, and the beauty you see in the world around you."

The hare paused, and I allowed the words to sink in. Prosperity was so much more than I had allowed it to be. It wasn't just about money—it was about the abundance of everything that made life rich: love, care, time, health, beauty, peace, joy, and fun. My mind raced through memories of moments when I felt truly prosperous—laughing with friends, feeling the warm sun on my face, having time to rest, enjoying the beauty of a sunset. None of those moments were tied to money.

"You must open your heart to all forms of prosperity," the hare said softly, "not just financial wealth, but the wealth of experiences, of emotions, of connection. True prosperity is limitless, and it is yours to receive if you allow it."

As the hare's words resonated within me, I felt a subtle shift, a sense of expansion. It was as if a door had been opened inside me, one that had always been there, but I had never noticed. I had been so focused on the material aspect of prosperity that I had overlooked the abundance that already filled my life.

"Tell me, how have you limited your idea of prosperity?" the hare asked, tilting its head slightly, as if it already knew the answer but wanted me to discover it for myself.

I took a deep breath, reflecting on the question. I realized that I had been fixated on the idea that prosperity was something I needed to chase, something that was out of reach unless I earned more, worked harder, or achieved more in the eyes of the world. I had limited prosperity to the size of my bank account, ignoring the richness of life already surrounding me.

"I've focused too much on money," I admitted, my voice barely a whisper. "I thought prosperity was something you earned, but now I see it's something much deeper."

The hare nodded, satisfied with my realization. It then spoke again, its voice gentle but firm.

"What does true prosperity look like to you?" it asked, urging me to explore the question further.

I closed my eyes and let the question settle. True prosperity, I realized, was about balance. It was about having enough time to spend with loved ones, enough health to enjoy life's pleasures, enough peace to rest easy at night, and enough joy to laugh freely. It was about living a life full of meaning and connection, not just one filled with material possessions.

"Now," the hare said, "it's time to set your intentions. If you are ready to invite all forms of prosperity into your life, you must be clear about what you wish to create."

With that, the hare instructed me to reflect on my deepest desires—the things I truly wanted to manifest in the next two months. I could feel the energy of the moment building, as if the universe itself was waiting for me to speak my wishes into existence.

"List your prosperity goals," the hare urged, "but not just financial ones. What do you want to create in your life? What will bring you love, joy, peace, and fulfillment?"

I thought carefully and then made my wishes. I could see them in my mind, vivid and full of possibility. The hare, sensing my clarity, gave me a final instruction.

"Take these wishes and make them real," it said. "Write them down with your non-dominant hand, for this will connect you to the intuitive part of yourself. Do this every day—ten times each morning and night. As you write, visualize your wishes coming true. See them as if they are already happening. The more you focus on them, the more energy you will give them, and they will come to life."

I nodded, understanding the importance of this practice. It was not just about writing words on paper—it was about giving life to my intentions, empowering them with my focus and attention.

"Remember," the hare said before it started to fade from my vision, "prosperity is always available to you, in every form. All you need to do is open yourself to receive it."

As the hare disappeared into the mist of my inner world, I felt a profound sense of peace. I opened my eyes and found myself back under the oak tree, the night sky twinkling with stars. I knew, deep within my soul, that my understanding of prosperity had forever changed. It was no longer something to chase—it was something to allow, something to embrace.

I whispered the hare's final words to myself, as if sealing them into my heart:

Affirmation

"I am open to receiving all forms of prosperity in my life."

The Hare said; Just wait for my whispers and what to do next!

I said "Thank you my Brother"

With that, I rose to my feet, ready to step into a life filled with the true meaning of prosperity—love, joy, health, beauty, peace, and yes, money too, but now as part of a much richer tapestry of abundance.

***

Hare whispered in my Dreams; For Releasing Resistance to Change, I suggest you speak to the Snake as your spirit animal guide. The snake is a powerful symbol of transformation, shedding old skin, and embracing new beginnings. It represents the release of resistance to change and the ability to flow with life's cycles. The snake teaches us to let go of old patterns and beliefs that no longer serve us, making it the perfect guide for releasing resistance and opening up to new possibilities.

In this chapter, the snake can help you understand how to let go of the fear and discomfort associated with change, and guide you to shed the old layers that are holding you back from true prosperity.

It takes more energy to hold on to resistance.

Drop all Significance; Do not tire yourself; Nothing means Nothing!

Chapter 2:

The Serpent's Wisdom – Releasing Resistance to Change

The night was cool, and the gentle hum of nature surrounded me as I sat beneath the same oak tree where I had previously met the hare. Tonight, I had returned to seek guidance on something that had been weighing heavily on my heart: change. More specifically, my resistance to it.

In my daily life, I had felt a constant undercurrent of resistance; resistance to new opportunities, resistance to letting go of old habits, resistance to change. It felt like a weight holding me down, keeping me from moving forward, from fully embracing the prosperity I desired. I knew it was time to address this, and once again, I called upon the spirit realm for guidance.

Closing my eyes, I took a deep breath, feeling the earth beneath me, grounding me as I began my journey inward. Slowly, the familiar Gates of Axis Mundi (the Tree of Life) of my inner world unfolded before me. I walked through the quiet, mist-laden forest, the trees swaying gently in the distance as I moved deeper into my journey.

As I walked, I felt the presence of my spirit animal guide—the hare—by my side. Its soft steps padded alongside me as if reminding me that I was never alone on this path. The hare's wisdom had guided me through understanding prosperity in all its forms, but tonight, it was time to meet another guide—the one who would help me release the resistance I had unknowingly held on to.

In the distance, I saw the flicker of movement, a long, sinuous form weaving gracefully through the grass. The hare nudged me gently, and I knew it was time to meet the snake, my spirit animal for transformation. The snake, ancient and wise, was a symbol of shedding old skin, of letting go, of embracing change.

I stood still as the snake slowly approached, its scales glistening in the soft moonlight. It circled around me, its movements calm and deliberate, as if waiting for me to acknowledge its presence.

"You seek to release resistance," the snake hissed softly, its voice both soothing and powerful. "You hold on tightly to what you know, but change is the only constant. It is time to shed the old and embrace the new."

I nodded, feeling the truth of the snake's words resonate within me. The snake's movements were fluid, effortless, reminding me of the flow of life, the way it constantly shifts and changes. And yet, here I was, stuck in my old patterns, afraid to move forward.

"Why do you resist change?" the snake asked, its eyes locking onto mine.

The question hung in the air, heavy and filled with meaning. I knew the answer, though I had never fully admitted it to myself. Fear. Fear of the unknown, fear of failure, fear of losing control. The comfort of what I knew, even if it wasn't serving me, felt safer than the uncertainty of change.

"You resist receiving as well," the snake continued. "You think you are managing, but in reality, you are blocking the flow of prosperity. Managing is not thriving. It is survival, and you are meant to thrive."

The snake's words cut through the fog in my mind. I had been telling myself that I was "managing" life, getting by, doing what was necessary to stay afloat. But deep down, I knew I wasn't thriving. I wasn't fully allowing prosperity in because I was too afraid to let go of what felt familiar, even if it wasn't truly fulfilling.

"In what areas of your life are you merely managing?" the snake asked, coiling itself around a rock, its eyes still locked on mine.

I closed my eyes and allowed the question to settle in my heart. The answers came quickly, clearer than I expected. In my career, I had been playing it safe, sticking with what I knew rather than pursuing the opportunities that excited me. In my relationships, I had been holding back, tolerating situations that no longer brought me joy. Even in my personal growth, I had been resisting the changes I needed to make to truly expand.

"I am managing in more areas than I realized," I whispered, the weight of that realization sinking in.

The snake nodded, its movements slow and deliberate. "To thrive, you must release your resistance. Change is not to be feared. It is a natural part of growth, of life. When you release resistance, you open yourself to new possibilities."

The snake's words were like a key unlocking a door within me. I had been resisting change because I had equated it with loss—loss of control, loss of comfort, loss of what I knew. But now I saw that change was not about losing; it was about gaining. Gaining new opportunities, new experiences, and new forms of prosperity that I couldn't even imagine yet.

"How would embracing change open new doors for prosperity?" the snake asked, its voice soft but insistent.

I thought about it. If I embraced change instead of fearing it, I could step into opportunities that aligned with my true desires. I could pursue the career paths that excited me, build relationships that truly nurtured me, and open myself to receiving in ways I had never allowed before. I could stop tolerating and start thriving.

"Change is the key to unlocking your prosperity," the snake said, slithering closer. "But it is up to you to take the first step. What are you willing to release?"

I felt the weight of the question. What was I willing to let go of in order to thrive? What old habits, beliefs, or fears had I been holding on to that were keeping me stuck?

"I am willing to release my fear of the unknown," I said slowly, feeling the truth of the words settle in my heart. "I am willing to release the need to control everything and to open myself to new possibilities."

The snake's eyes softened, and it uncoiled itself from the rock, coming to rest at my feet. "You are ready," it whispered. "But remember, change does not happen all at once. It happens in small steps. Start by taking one small action toward thriving, and watch as the doors of prosperity open for you." So just "Take a small action today," the snake instructed, "and see how it shifts your energy. When you release resistance, you create space for prosperity to flow in ways you never thought possible."

I nodded, knowing that the snake's wisdom was exactly what I needed. I had been resisting change because it felt overwhelming, but now I understood that it didn't have to be. I could start small—one step, one action, one decision at a time.

I knew what I had to do. When I returned from this journey, I would take that first small step. I would stop managing and start thriving. I would release my fear and open myself to the infinite possibilities that change could bring.

The snake began to move again, slowly retreating into the grass. Its presence left me with a sense of calm, a deep knowing that I was ready to embrace change, to release the old and welcome the new.

As the snake disappeared into the distance, the hare returned, its eyes warm and knowing.

"Remember," the hare said softly, "prosperity is not just about receiving—it's about allowing. When you allow change, you allow prosperity in all its forms to flow into your life."

I smiled, feeling a deep sense of peace. I knew now that I was ready. I was ready to release my resistance, to let go of the old, and to open myself fully to the abundance that awaited me.

I whispered the affirmation to myself, sealing the lesson into my heart:

Affirmation:

"I release all resistance to change and open myself to new possibilities."

With that, I opened my eyes, back under the oak tree, the night air cool against my skin. The stars twinkled above, and I felt lighter, freer, as if a great weight had been lifted. I was ready for change, ready to thrive, and ready to welcome all forms of prosperity into my life.

Growth Work for Home Play:

Reflection:

Write down areas in your life where you are tolerating or “managing” instead of thriving. Reflect on "what might happen if you embraced change in those areas?"

Action Step:

Take a small action today to shift from managing to thriving in one area of your life. One Action may start the ball rolling, Whether it’s pursuing a new opportunity, letting go of an old habit, or embracing something new, notice how this small shift begins to open up new doors for you.

- Identify what will be that One Action.

As I stood and walked back home, I felt a sense of excitement. The doors to prosperity were no longer locked. They were wide open, waiting for me to step through. And step through I would.

Hare whispered in my Dreams; For The Power of Focus, the ideal spirit animal guide would be the Hawk. The hawk is known for its sharp vision and ability to focus intensely on its prey, even from great distances. It symbolizes clarity, perspective, and the power of honing in on what truly matters. The hawk teaches us to see the bigger picture while also concentrating on the small, important details, which aligns perfectly with the theme of focusing on abundance in your life.

In this chapter, the hawk can guide you in understanding how to direct your energy and attention toward what you want to manifest, helping you to stay clear, purposeful, and unwavering in your focus.

Future depends on how present are you Now.

Chapter 3:

The Hawk's Vision – The Power of Focus

The morning sun bathed the landscape in a golden glow, illuminating the path ahead as I returned to my familiar oak tree. Today felt different—lighter, as if the air was clearer, and the possibilities of the day were wide open. I had come seeking wisdom on something that had been swirling in my mind: focus.

I had spent so much of my life focusing on what was missing—what I didn't have, what wasn't working, the gaps, the scarcity. It had become a constant background noise, and I knew it was shaping my reality in ways I wasn't fully aware of. Now, I wanted to shift that.

Closing my eyes, I breathed deeply, allowing my consciousness to drift into my shamanic journey. The familiar mist enveloped me as I walked deeper into the inner realms, searching for the guidance I needed. Beside me, as always, was the hare, its quiet presence grounding me as I moved forward. Today, however, I knew another guide awaited me.

As the mist cleared, I found myself standing at the edge of a wide, open plain. The sky stretched endlessly above, a vast canvas of blue and gold. I felt a stirring in the air, a soft breeze that carried with it a sense of clarity. And then, I saw it—a majestic hawk, soaring high above, its wings gliding effortlessly on the currents of the wind. It circled slowly, its sharp eyes scanning the ground below, every movement deliberate, every focus precise.

I watched the hawk, mesmerized by its grace and focus. There was something deeply powerful in the way it moved—calm, yet alert. The hawk circled lower and lower until it landed on a nearby rock, its eyes locked onto mine with an intensity that took my breath away.

"You seek to understand focus," the hawk said, its voice clear and direct, like an arrow aimed at its target.

I nodded. "Yes," I replied softly. "I feel like I've been focusing on the wrong things—on scarcity, on lack. And I know it's affecting my life. How do I shift my focus to abundance?"

The hawk's eyes narrowed slightly, as if studying me. It took a moment before responding.

"Whatever you focus on grows," it said simply. "This is a truth that governs all of life. Whether you focus on abundance or scarcity, you will create more of it. Your energy flows to where your attention goes."

I felt a deep sense of recognition as the hawk spoke. I had heard similar words before, but never had they resonated as deeply as they did now. The hawk's words weren't just advice—they were a profound truth.

"Look at me," the hawk continued, its wings spreading slightly as if to demonstrate. "When I fly, my eyes are fixed on my goal, my prey. I see the bigger picture—the landscape, the sky, the horizon—but my focus is sharp. I do not waver. I do not allow distractions; And because of that, I succeed in what I pursue."

The hawk's eyes bore into mine, and I felt the weight of its message. My own focus had been scattered, torn between the fears of not having enough and the desires for more. I had been so consumed by what I lacked that I had forgotten to truly focus on what I wanted to create.

"What do you focus on more?" the hawk asked, its voice steady. "Scarcity or abundance?"

The question hit me like a wave. I had to admit the truth. I had spent far too much time focusing on scarcity—on what was missing, what I didn't have, the gaps in my life. And as the hawk had said, whatever I focused on, I was creating more of.

"Scarcity," I whispered, my voice tinged with regret. "I've been focusing on scarcity."

The hawk tilted its head slightly, as if it had expected that answer. "Then that is what you will create. But you have the power to shift your focus. It is your choice, always."

I nodded, I had the power to change my focus, toward what I wanted to create, rather than what I feared.

"Shifting your focus to abundance," the hawk continued, "is not a one-time decision. It is a practice. Every day, you must choose where to place your attention. Abundance is everywhere—love, joy, opportunities—but you must be willing to see it. If you focus only on lack, you blind yourself to the possibilities that surround you."

The hawk's words were like a beacon, showing me the way forward. It wasn't about denying that scarcity existed—it was about choosing to focus on the abundance that was already present in my life.

"How can shifting your focus to abundance change your reality?" the hawk asked, its eyes never leaving mine.

I thought about it. If I focused on abundance—on the love, opportunities, and joy already in my life—I could create more of it. I could shift from feeling like life was happening to me, to feeling empowered to create the life I wanted. I could stop seeing obstacles and start seeing possibilities. I could invite prosperity into my life by aligning my thoughts, energy, and actions with abundance.

"Focusing on abundance will change everything," I said, feeling the truth of my words resonate deep within me.

The hawk nodded, satisfied with my realization. "Then it is time for you to begin."

With that, the hawk spread its wings and flew into the air, circling high above, its eyes scanning the landscape with laser-like precision. I knew what I needed to do—I needed to train my mind to focus on abundance, just as the hawk focused on its prey.

"Shift your focus," the hawk called out from above. "Write down the areas in your life where you focus on lack. Then, consciously choose to focus on abundance. Practice it every day."

I nodded, committing to the task. As I watched the hawk soar higher, I felt the presence of the hare beside me again, a gentle reminder of the wisdom I had already learned on this journey.

"Each day, write down three things you are grateful for," the hare added, its voice soft and nurturing. "Gratitude is the key to training your mind to focus on abundance. The more you focus on what you have, the more you will attract."

The hare's words blended with the hawk's wisdom, and I understood the practice I needed to adopt. Gratitude was a powerful tool to shift focus—it allowed me to see abundance even in the smallest of things.

"I will," I promised, my heart full of determination. "I will focus on abundance, and I will practice gratitude every day."

With that commitment, the hawk soared higher into the sky, disappearing into the golden horizon. The hare lingered by my side for a moment longer, its presence comforting, before it, too, faded into the mist of my journey.

As I opened my eyes, back under the oak tree, I felt a renewed sense of clarity and purpose. The message was clear: Whatever I focused on would grow. It was up to me to decide whether I wanted to focus on scarcity or abundance. And from this moment on, I chose abundance.

I whispered the affirmation aloud, feeling its power resonate deep within me:

Affirmation:
"I focus on abundance, and I attract more of it into my life."

Growth Work for Home Play:

Focus Shift:
Write down the areas in your life where you focus on lack. Reflect on how this focus has shaped your reality. Then, consciously choose to focus on abundance in those areas.
Ask yourself: What is already abundant in my life? How can I see more of it?

Gratitude Practice:
Each day, write down three things you are grateful for. It could be as simple as a kind gesture, a moment of peace, or something you received unexpectedly. This practice will train your mind to focus on the abundance that already exists in your life.

Discussion Points:

What do you focus on more in your life—scarcity or abundance?

How can shifting your focus to abundance change your financial and overall reality?

As I stood and made my way back home, I felt lighter, freer. I now had the tools to change my reality, to focus on the abundance that was already present in my life, and to invite even more into my world. With the wisdom of the hawk and the hare guiding me, I was ready to create a life filled with prosperity.

Hare whispered in my Dreams; For Acknowledging Your Power of Choice, the ideal spirit animal guide would be the Wolf. The wolf represents instinct, intelligence, and the power of decision-making. Wolves are known for their ability to balance independence with cooperation, making powerful choices for the benefit of the pack while also trusting their instincts. The wolf teaches us to trust our inner wisdom and make empowered decisions that align with our path.

In this chapter, the wolf can guide you to recognize that your life is shaped by your choices, and it can help you embrace the power of making decisions from a place of strength and confidence. The wolf's wisdom will help you acknowledge your past choices and empower you to make new ones that lead to greater prosperity.

Every thought you entertain creates your reality

You can walk with them and still follow your knowing

Chapter 4:

The Wolf's Path – Acknowledging Your Power of Choice

The forest was quieter than usual as I prepared for my next shamanic journey. The breeze was soft, and the sky, a gentle gray, seemed to mirror the uncertainty I felt within. The more I ventured into the realms of my inner world, the more I uncovered about myself—my patterns, my habits, my beliefs. But now, something deeper had surfaced: the power of choice.

I knew that my life was shaped by the choices I made, but there were so many decisions, large and small, that had led me to where I was now. Some I was proud of, others weighed on me with the regret of roads not taken. How much control did I truly have over my reality? How could I begin to make choices that would truly lead me toward prosperity?

I closed my eyes, sitting beneath the oak tree that had become my grounding place. I breathed deeply, feeling the earth beneath me, and allowed myself to drift once more into the Gates of Axis Mundi (the Tree of Life) of my shamanic journey.

As I stepped into this familiar realm, I felt the presence of the hare beside me, its soft paws barely making a sound as it walked alongside me. The hare had been my companion on many journeys, always offering gentle wisdom. But today, I knew I needed a guide who would help me understand the power and responsibility of choice—a guide who could help me navigate the often daunting paths of decision-making.

We walked in silence until we reached a clearing. The air was still, and I sensed I was on the verge of something important. Then, from the shadows of the trees, a figure emerged—a sleek, powerful wolf. Its fur was a mix of silver and gray, its eyes sharp and full of knowing. The wolf moved with a calm confidence, every step deliberate, every movement purposeful. This was the spirit I had called for—one who could teach me about the power of choice.

The wolf approached and stood before me, its gaze never wavering.

"You have come to understand the power of choice," the wolf said, its voice deep and steady. "Every path you walk is a choice, and every choice shapes your reality."

I nodded, feeling the weight of the wolf's words settle in my heart. The truth was undeniable. My life, my financial reality, my relationships—they were all the result of choices I had made, both consciously and unconsciously.

"Do you understand the choices that have brought you here?" the wolf asked, its eyes piercing through me as if seeing into my soul.

I paused, reflecting on the question. I knew there were choices I had made—some out of fear, others out of necessity. There were also choices I hadn't made, paths I hadn't taken because I was too afraid of the unknown or too attached to the comfort of the familiar. Slowly, I began to realize that my current reality, especially my financial situation, was the sum of all these decisions.

"What choices have shaped your current financial reality?" the wolf pressed.

I closed my eyes and allowed the memories to surface. I thought about the times I had settled for less, choosing security over risk, comfort over growth. I thought about the opportunities I had passed by, telling myself I wasn't ready or wasn't deserving. I had made choices out of scarcity, out of fear, and these choices had built the foundation of my current financial reality.

"I've made choices that were rooted in fear," I admitted, my voice barely above a whisper. "I've chosen to stay safe instead of reaching for more. And I see now how those choices have shaped where I am."

The wolf's gaze softened slightly, though its eyes remained focused. "You have the power to choose differently now," it said. "Every moment presents a new choice. The power is always yours, even when you feel stuck or trapped. It is not the past choices that define you—it is the choices you make from this point forward."

The wolf's words hit me deeply. It wasn't too late. I could choose differently. I could reclaim my power by acknowledging that, moving forward, every choice was an opportunity to create a new reality.

"How does owning your choices empower you to change your future?" the wolf asked, tilting its head slightly as if inviting me to reflect more deeply.

I realized that by owning my choices, I could no longer play the victim in my own life. By taking responsibility for my past decisions, I could stop blaming external circumstances or other people. I could step into my power and decide—right now—to make better, more empowered choices. This was the key to transforming my relationship with prosperity. If I had the power to choose, then I had the power to create the future I wanted.

"It empowers me," I answered, my voice stronger now. "It means I'm not a victim of circumstance. I can change my future by changing my choices."

The wolf nodded approvingly. "Exactly. Prosperity is not something that happens to you—it is something you choose. Every thought, every action, every decision is a choice that shapes your reality. The question is, what will you choose next?"

The question hung in the air, filled with possibility. What would I choose next? How would I make decisions moving forward? I understood now that even the smallest choices could have a profound impact on my life, especially when made with intention.

"Now," the wolf said, its voice low and firm, "it is time for you to reflect on your past choices and commit to making empowered decisions moving forward."

I nodded, understanding the task before me. The wolf stepped closer, its presence strong and reassuring.

"You will reflect on the choices you've made that have affected your financial reality," the wolf continued, "but you will not judge them. You will simply acknowledge them. Then, you will choose to make better choices from this moment on."

I felt the power of the wolf's words settle deep within me. There was no need for judgment, only acknowledgment. I had made choices that led me here, but now I had the power to make new ones, better ones.

"Take a small step toward empowerment," the wolf instructed. "Commit to making one empowered financial decision this week. It doesn't have to be a big decision, but it must be made from a place of clarity, not fear."

The wolf's wisdom was clear and precise, and I knew what I needed to do. When I returned from this journey, I would take the time to reflect on my past choices, but more importantly, I would commit to making an empowered decision—one that would move me toward the prosperity I desired.

The wolf began to circle me, its presence a constant reminder of the power within me. "Remember," it said softly, "you are never powerless. Every moment is a choice. And with each choice, you have the power to create the reality you want."

As the wolf's words resonated through me, I felt a surge of energy, a deep sense of empowerment that I hadn't felt before. I wasn't at the mercy of life's circumstances—I was the creator of my own path. I had the power to choose, and that power was mine to wield.

The wolf stepped back, its eyes watching me intently. "You know what to do," it said, before slowly retreating into the shadows of the forest.

I stood there, feeling the weight of the lesson I had just learned. The hare, who had been quietly observing, stepped forward, its eyes kind and understanding.

"The power of choice is always with you," the hare said gently. "Use it wisely, and you will create the prosperity you seek."

With a final nod, the hare disappeared into the mist, leaving me standing alone in the clearing, but I no longer felt alone. I felt empowered, ready to take responsibility for my choices and ready to create a new reality.

I opened my eyes, back under the oak tree, the morning sun warming my skin. I whispered the affirmation to myself, sealing the lesson into my heart:

Affirmation:
"I create my reality and have the power to change it."

Growth Work for Home Play:

Reflection:
Write down the choices you've made that have affected your financial reality.
Acknowledge these choices without judgment, and reflect on how they have shaped your life.
Now, ask yourself how you can make better choices moving forward.

Empowerment Exercise:
Commit to making one empowered financial decision this week. It could be as simple as choosing to save a small amount of money, invest in something that aligns with your goals, or say no to an expense that doesn't serve you. Make this decision from a place of clarity and intention, not fear.

Discussion Points:

1. What choices have shaped your current financial reality?
2. How does owning your choices empower you to change your future?

As I stood and walked back home, I felt a new sense of clarity and confidence. The wolf had shown me the path, and now it was up to me to walk it. Every choice was a step, and each step had the power to transform my life. With the wisdom of the wolf and the hare guiding me, I knew I had the power to create the prosperity I desired.

Hare whispered in my Dreams; Money as Energy, the ideal spirit animal guide would be the Eagle. The eagle represents clarity, vision, and higher perspectives. It flies high above the world, seeing the bigger picture, and embodies the freedom and flow that money as energy symbolizes. The eagle teaches us to rise above limiting beliefs, view money not as a fixed object but as a fluid energy, and understand how to channel it effectively in our lives.

In this chapter, the eagle can guide you to see money as energy that flows in and out, much like the wind beneath its wings. It will help you understand the concept of money beyond material possession and see it as a resource to be used, not hoarded. The eagle's wisdom will assist you in aligning your mindset with abundance and flow.

Chapter 5: The Eagle's Flight – Money as Energy

It was early morning, and the first rays of sunlight streamed through the trees as I prepared for another shamanic journey. Today, the air was crisp and light, filled with the promise of clarity and revelation. I had been contemplating the idea of money as energy, a concept that both intrigued and challenged me. Money had always felt like something heavy—something serious, even stressful. But if it was energy, if it could be played with and manipulated, then I needed to learn how to flow with it instead of feeling weighed down by it.

I closed my eyes and took a deep breath, feeling the familiar warmth of the earth beneath me as I drifted into the misty realm of my inner world. As I journeyed deeper, I knew I was about to encounter a guide who could help me see money differently—through the lens of energy and playfulness.

The hare, my constant companion, hopped beside me as I moved through the landscape, always present, always offering gentle wisdom. But today, I could sense the presence of another, waiting for me to arrive.

As the mist parted, I found myself standing on a cliff's edge, the vast sky stretching endlessly before me. The wind stirred, carrying with it a sense of freedom and expansiveness. I knew this was the place where I would meet my next spirit guide.

High above, I saw a magnificent eagle, soaring effortlessly through the sky. Its wings stretched wide, gliding on the currents of the wind with grace and ease. The eagle circled above, its sharp eyes scanning the world below, seeing everything with clarity and precision. I felt a sense of awe watching it—this powerful bird that moved with such lightness, such mastery of the air.

The eagle descended gracefully, landing on a rock near me. Its presence was commanding, yet there was a lightness to it, a freedom in the way it held itself. The eagle's eyes met mine, and I felt as though it could see straight into my soul, into my deepest beliefs about money, abundance, and energy.

"You have come to understand money as energy," the eagle said, its voice strong and clear, like the wind itself.

I nodded, my heart open to the wisdom that was about to unfold. "Yes," I said softly. "I've always seen money as something heavy, something serious. But I want to understand how to treat it as energy, how to play with it and allow it to flow more freely into my life."

The eagle's eyes remained fixed on me, its gaze unwavering. "Money is energy," it said. "It is neither heavy nor light—it becomes what you make of it. If you see it as a burden, it will feel heavy. If you see it as playful, it will flow with ease. The key to prosperity is not in controlling money but in mastering the way you engage with it, just as I master the wind."

I felt the truth of the eagle's words settle within me. The way I had been viewing money—as something scarce, something to be controlled—was the very thing that had been blocking its flow. I had been holding onto it too tightly, fearful of losing it, and in doing so, I had created a sense of heaviness around it. But if money was energy, then it could be fluid, like the air beneath the eagle's wings.

"How do you currently view money?" the eagle asked, its voice piercing through my thoughts. "As something heavy or something light and playful?"

I took a deep breath, reflecting on the question. "I've viewed it as something heavy," I admitted, my voice barely a whisper. "Something that brings stress, something that's hard to come by."

The eagle tilted its head slightly, as if considering my answer. "Then that is what you will continue to create," it said simply. "Whatever you believe about money will shape how it flows in your life. But if you are ready to see it differently, to play with it, you can change the way it moves in and out of your reality."

I felt a spark of hope at the eagle's words. I was ready to see money differently. I was ready to engage with it as energy, to release the heaviness I had associated with it for so long.

"How can you play with the energy of money?" the eagle asked, its sharp eyes watching me closely.

The question stirred something within me. Play with money? It was such a foreign concept to me—money had always felt serious, something to be managed, not something to play with. But now, standing before the eagle, I realized that this belief was exactly what had been limiting me.

"I don't know," I said honestly. "But I want to learn."

The eagle's eyes softened slightly, and it spread its wings, lifting into the air for a moment before settling back down, as if demonstrating the ease with which it moved through the world.

"Watch how I fly," the eagle said. "I do not struggle against the wind, nor do I try to control it. I move with it, using its energy to carry me. Money is no different. It is energy that flows in and out of your life. You cannot control it, but you can direct it, just as I direct my flight. When you treat money with lightness, when you play with it, it will flow to you more easily."

I watched the eagle, understanding its message more clearly than ever. It wasn't about controlling money or holding onto it out of fear. It was about allowing it to flow, trusting that it would come and go as part of a natural rhythm. And the more I played with it—investing it in things that brought me joy, giving freely without fear—the more it would return to me.

"Begin by shifting your view of money," the eagle instructed. "See it as something light, something playful. Write down the ways in which you can start to engage with money playfully, without stress or fear."

I nodded, committing to the task. I could already think of a few ways I could shift my relationship with money—investing in things that brought me joy, allowing myself to spend on experiences that made me feel abundant, rather than constantly worrying about saving every penny. I could play with money, just as I played with other forms of energy.

"Now," the eagle said, its voice lowering slightly, "close your eyes and visualize money as energy. See it flowing into your life with ease, like the wind beneath my wings."

I did as the eagle instructed, closing my eyes and breathing deeply. I imagined money as a shimmering energy, light and fluid, flowing into my life effortlessly. I saw it moving through me, in and out, without tension or fear. It felt expansive, freeing. The more I visualized it, the more I realized that money truly was energy—it wasn't something to be grasped tightly but something to be engaged with playfully and wisely.

After a few moments, I opened my eyes, feeling lighter, as though a weight had been lifted.

"You are beginning to understand," the eagle said, its eyes gleaming with approval. "Money will flow to you when you stop holding onto it with fear. Play with it, use it to create joy, and trust that it will return to you in ways you cannot yet imagine."

I nodded, my heart filled with gratitude for the eagle's wisdom. I had been carrying the weight of scarcity for too long, but now I understood that money was not something to be feared or controlled. It was energy, and like all energy, it could be directed and shaped through my thoughts, my actions, and my playfulness.

"Remember," the eagle said as it spread its wings once more, ready to take flight, "money is energy, and you are a master at playing with it."

With that, the eagle lifted off into the sky, soaring effortlessly into the horizon. I watched it fly, feeling a deep sense of freedom within myself. I knew now that I had the power to change my relationship with money, to treat it with lightness and play, and to allow it to flow into my life with ease.

The hare appeared beside me once again, its presence comforting and grounding. It nudged me gently, as if to remind me of the journey we had shared, and of the lessons I had learned.

"You have the power to create prosperity," the hare said softly. "When you treat money as energy, it becomes something fluid, something playful. Let go of the fear, and watch how it flows into your life."

I smiled, feeling the truth of the hare's words. I whispered the affirmation to myself, sealing the lesson into my heart:

Affirmation
"Money is energy, and I am a master at playing with it."

Growth Work for Home Play:

Energy Play:
Write down ways in which you can begin to play with money instead of viewing it as stressful or heavy. For example, invest in something that brings you joy, or spend on experiences that make you feel abundant. Notice how shifting your energy around money begins to change how it flows into your life.

Visualization Exercise:
Close your eyes and imagine money as energy that you can mold and shape. Picture it flowing easily into your life, light and abundant. Practice this visualization daily to train your mind to see money as something fluid and playful.

Discussion Points:

1. How do you currently view money: as something heavy or something light and playful?
2. How can you play with the energy of money to attract more of it?

As I stood and began my walk home, I felt a deep sense of lightness and possibility. With the wisdom of the eagle soaring in my heart, I understood that I had the power to shift my relationship with money by treating it as energy—something fluid, playful, and abundant.

- How can you play with the energy of money to attract more of it?

By engaging with money in a lighter, more playful way, you release the tight grip of fear and scarcity, allowing it to flow more freely into your life. You can start by shifting your perspective from seeing money as a finite resource to seeing it as a tool for joy and creation. Consider how you can make decisions that align with fun, joy, and investment in your happiness—whether that's treating yourself to something that brings you pleasure, investing in your personal growth, or giving freely to others. Each playful interaction with money opens the door to new opportunities for abundance. By focusing on how money can create more joy, you shift the energy and begin to attract more of it effortlessly.

Hare whispered in my Dreams; Releasing Judgments About Money, the ideal spirit animal guide would be the Owl. The owl is a symbol of wisdom, intuition, and seeing beyond illusions. It represents the ability to see through the darkness and uncover hidden truths, making it an ideal guide for addressing and releasing judgments. The owl can help you recognize the limiting beliefs and judgments you hold about money, guiding you to let go of those false perceptions and embrace a clearer, more empowered relationship with prosperity.

In this chapter, the owl's wisdom will assist you in seeing beyond societal or personal judgments about wealth and money, helping you navigate the shadows of fear and misconceptions to reach a place of clarity and openness to receiving abundance.

Chapter 6: The Owl's Insight – Releasing Judgments About Money

The moon was full tonight, casting its silver glow across the landscape as I prepared for my next shamanic journey. The air felt different—thicker, perhaps heavier—as if it carried the weight of something unseen. I had been thinking a lot about judgments, especially the ones I held about money. Deep down, I knew they were blocking my flow of prosperity, keeping me from receiving with ease. But how could I release them? How could I untangle the web of beliefs that had been with me for so long?

I closed my eyes and took a deep breath, grounding myself as I slipped into the familiar mist of my inner world. This time, I knew the journey would be different. The judgments I held about money were like shadows that lingered in the corners of my mind, and tonight, I was ready to confront them.

The hare, ever my companion, appeared beside me as I walked deeper into the misty forest. Its presence was calm and reassuring, reminding me that I was never alone in these journeys. But tonight, I sensed that I would need a new guide—one who could help me see clearly in the darkness, who could help me uncover the hidden beliefs that were holding me back.

As the mist cleared, I found myself standing at the edge of a dark, dense forest. The trees stretched high into the sky, their branches forming a canopy that blocked out most of the moonlight. It was here, in the shadows, that I would meet my guide. And then, from the depths of the forest, I heard it—the soft, haunting call of an owl.

I looked up, searching the trees, and there it was—perched high on a branch, its large eyes glowing in the moonlight. The owl stared down at me with an intensity that sent shivers through my spine. It was as if the owl could see straight through me, into the deepest parts of my mind where my judgments about money resided.

The owl spread its wings and glided silently down to a low branch, closer to where I stood. Its gaze was unrelenting, wise, and knowing. This was the guide I had come to meet—the one who could help me see beyond the illusions I had created.

"You have come to release your judgments about money," the owl said, its voice soft but powerful. "You see money as something separate from you, something to be judged, and in doing so, you block its flow."

I nodded, feeling the truth of the owl's words resonate deep within me. For so long, I had held onto beliefs about money—some I had inherited from others, some I had created myself. I had seen money as scarce, as something that was hard to come by. I had judged wealth as something only a few could attain, and I had viewed those with money through the lens of envy or suspicion. But now, standing before the owl, I knew it was time to release these judgments.

"What judgments have you held about money?" the owl asked, its large eyes never leaving mine.

I took a deep breath and allowed the memories to surface. I thought about the things I had heard growing up—phrases like "money doesn't grow on trees" or "people with money are greedy." These beliefs had shaped how I viewed wealth and how I interacted with it. I had been taught to fear not having enough, and at the same time, I had been conditioned to distrust those who had plenty.

"I've judged money as something scarce," I admitted, my voice barely a whisper. "I've seen it as something that is hard to attain, and I've judged those who have it."

The owl tilted its head slightly, as if considering my words. "And how have these judgments limited your ability to receive prosperity?"

I thought about it. Every time I had judged money as scarce, I had reinforced that belief in my reality. I had struggled financially because I had believed that money was hard to come by. And every time I judged others for their wealth, I had pushed prosperity away from myself, as if telling the universe that I didn't want to be like them. These judgments had created a barrier, one that I hadn't even been fully aware of.

"They've limited me in so many ways," I said slowly, the weight of the realization settling in. "I haven't allowed myself to receive because I've believed that I'm not worthy of it, or that money is something that should be judged."

The owl's eyes softened slightly, and it leaned forward, its gaze still sharp but filled with understanding. "Money is energy," it said, echoing the lesson I had learned from the eagle. "It carries no inherent judgment, no morality. It simply flows where it is allowed to flow. But your judgments have blocked that flow. You have placed walls around your ability to receive, and those walls are made of your beliefs."

I felt a wave of emotion rise within me. The owl was right. I had been holding onto these judgments for so long that I had forgotten that money, like any energy, was neutral. It wasn't inherently good or bad—it just was. And I had the power to decide how I wanted to engage with it.

"What must I do to release these judgments?" I asked, my voice filled with both hope and vulnerability.

The owl's eyes gleamed in the moonlight, its feathers ruffling slightly in the breeze. "You must first acknowledge them," it said. "Write them down, bring them into the light. And then, one by one, release them. Each day, choose a judgment to let go of. Visualize yourself opening up to money without judgment, allowing it to flow into your life as easily as the wind flows through the trees."

I nodded, understanding the task ahead of me. It wasn't enough to simply recognize these judgments—I had to actively release them. I had to train my mind to see money not as something to be feared or judged but as something that could flow into my life with ease.

"Begin by writing down the judgments you hold," the owl instructed. "Every belief, every thought that has shaped your relationship with money. And then, release them. One by one."

I knew what I had to do. When I returned from this journey, I would take the time to write down every judgment I held about money—every belief that had kept me stuck in a cycle of scarcity and fear. And then, each day, I would choose to release one. I would visualize myself opening up to the flow of prosperity, free from the weight of judgment.

"Remember," the owl said, its voice soft but firm, "money is neutral. It is neither good nor bad. It is energy, and like all energy, it will flow where it is welcomed. Release your judgments, and you will open yourself to receiving it with ease."

The owl's words filled me with a sense of calm and clarity. I had been carrying the weight of these judgments for far too long, and now, with the owl's guidance, I knew I had the power to release them. I had the power to change my relationship with money, to allow it to flow into my life without fear or judgment.

The owl spread its wings, ready to take flight. But before it left, it spoke one final time.

"Affirm this truth," it said. "Speak it aloud, and let it become your reality: 'I release all judgments about money and open myself to receiving it with ease.'"

I repeated the affirmation, feeling the weight of my old beliefs begin to lift:

Affirmation:
"I release all judgments about money and open myself to receiving it with ease."

With that, the owl soared into the night sky, disappearing into the darkness with a silent grace. The hare, still beside me, nudged me gently, reminding me that I was on the right path—that with each step, I was moving closer to the prosperity I sought.

As I opened my eyes, back beneath the oak tree, I felt lighter, freer. I knew now that the judgments I had held about money were not truths—they were simply beliefs that I had the power to change. And with each belief I released, I would open myself to the flow of abundance that had always been available to me.

Growth Work for Home Play:

Money Beliefs:
Write down all the judgments you hold about money. These could be beliefs you've inherited from others, experiences you've had, or thoughts you've created. Reflect on how each of these judgments has affected your financial reality.

Releasing Exercise:
Each day, choose one judgment to release. Visualize yourself letting go of this belief, and imagine money flowing into your life without any barriers. Practice this until you feel free from the weight of judgment.

Discussion Points:

1. *What judgments have you held about money?*
2. *How have these judgments limited your ability to receive prosperity?*

As I stood and made my way back home, I whispered the affirmation once more, feeling the power of the owl's wisdom in my heart:

"I release all judgments about money and open myself to receiving it with ease."

Hare whispered in my Dreams; Opening Up to Opportunities, the ideal spirit animal guide would be the Fox. The fox is known for its adaptability, cleverness, and ability to seize opportunities in unexpected ways. It teaches us to be aware of our surroundings, to think quickly, and to take advantage of opportunities when they arise, even if they appear hidden or unconventional. The fox represents the ability to move with agility and grace through life, opening up to new paths and possibilities with confidence.

In this chapter, the fox can guide you to become more aware of the opportunities around you and help you trust your instincts when taking action on them. The fox's wisdom will encourage you to stay alert, adaptable, and ready to embrace new prospects with courage and creativity.

Chapter 7: The Fox's Wisdom – Opening Up to Opportunities

The day had just begun, and the air was alive with the fresh scent of dew and possibility. I stood under the familiar oak tree, I had been learning how to release my judgments about money, treat it as energy, and shift my focus to abundance, but something still felt out of reach. It was as if there were opportunities waiting for me just beyond my line of sight, but I wasn't seeing them.

Today, I sought guidance on how to open up to the opportunities around me—opportunities that I knew were there, but somehow I had been missing. Whether out of fear or a mindset focused on scarcity, I had often overlooked or dismissed the chances that life had offered me. But now, I was ready to see things differently.

I closed my eyes and took a deep breath, centering myself as I began my shamanic journey. As the mist rose around me, I felt the familiar presence of the hare by my side, always gentle, always watchful.

As I walked deeper into the mist, I found myself standing at the edge of a dense forest. The trees towered above me, their branches weaving together to form a canopy of green and gold. The forest felt alive with movement, and in the shadows, I sensed something watching me. My heart quickened in anticipation. This was the guide I had come to meet—the one who could help me see the hidden paths and opportunities that were waiting for me.

Suddenly, a fox appeared, darting gracefully from the trees. Its fur gleamed in the dappled sunlight, a rich blend of russet and white, and its eyes sparkled with intelligence and mischief. The fox moved with quiet confidence, its every step deliberate yet light, as if it knew exactly where it was going, even when the path wasn't clear.

The fox circled me once, its eyes studying me intently before sitting down at the edge of the clearing. It waited patiently, as though giving me time to gather my thoughts.

"You seek to open yourself to opportunities," the fox said, its voice smooth and playful, much like its movements. "But you are often too focused on what is missing to see what is right in front of you."

I nodded, feeling the truth of the fox's words. I had been so caught up in my fears—fears of scarcity, of not having enough—that I hadn't been able to see the abundance of opportunities that had come my way. I had let chances slip by, dismissing them as too risky, or not recognizing them for what they were.

"Opportunities are all around you," the fox continued, "but you miss them because you are too focused on what you think you lack. It is time to shift your gaze, to see the opportunities that are already here, waiting for you to seize them."

The fox's eyes gleamed as it spoke, and I realized that this creature was a master of opportunity. The fox, with its cleverness and agility, knew how to move swiftly, how to adapt to its surroundings, and how to make the most of every situation. If anyone could teach me how to recognize and act on opportunities, it was the fox.

"What opportunities have you overlooked?" the fox asked, its gaze locking onto mine.

I closed my eyes and allowed the memories to surface. I thought about the job offers I had turned down because I was afraid of change. I remembered the financial investments I had avoided, telling myself I wasn't ready or that they were too risky. And then there were the personal opportunities—the relationships I hadn't pursued, the creative projects I hadn't followed through on, all because I had been too focused on what could go wrong.

"I've overlooked so many," I admitted, my voice heavy with regret. "I've let fear keep me from seeing what was right in front of me."

The fox's eyes softened slightly, and it tilted its head as if encouraging me to look deeper.

"And how can you open yourself up to opportunities without fear?" the fox asked, its voice gentle but probing.

I took a deep breath, reflecting on the question. How could I stop letting fear control my decisions? How could I begin to see opportunities for what they were—chances to grow, to prosper, to step into a more abundant life? The answer came to me slowly but clearly: I had to trust myself. I had to trust that I was capable of handling whatever came my way, that I didn't have to be perfect or have all the answers before taking action. I just had to be willing to try.

"I need to trust myself," I said, my voice filled with new resolve. "I need to stop letting fear hold me back and start embracing opportunities as they come."

The fox nodded, its eyes gleaming with approval. "Exactly. Opportunities do not come with guarantees, but they come with possibilities. It is up to you to decide whether to seize them or let them pass by."

The fox stood up, its movements graceful and sure. "Begin by writing down the opportunities you have overlooked," it said, circling me once more. "Acknowledge them, but do not dwell on them. Then, start opening your eyes to the opportunities around you now. Keep a journal for the next week, and every day, write down any opportunity you notice—no matter how small."

I nodded, understanding the task before me. It wasn't just about looking for the big, obvious opportunities—it was about being alert, open, and adaptable to even the smallest chances that could lead to something greater. Just like the fox, I needed to stay light on my feet, ready to move and shift when the time was right.

"Remember," the fox said, its voice soft but filled with meaning, "opportunities are everywhere. You just need to be open to seeing them."

With that, the fox darted into the trees, disappearing into the shadows as swiftly as it had appeared. The hare remained by my side, its presence steady and comforting.

"Opportunities are often hidden in the places you least expect," the hare said, its voice gentle. "But when you open yourself up to seeing them, they will reveal themselves to you. Trust in your ability to recognize and seize them."

I smiled, feeling a new sense of excitement bubbling up within me. I whispered the affirmation aloud, sealing it into my heart:

Affirmation:
"I am open to all opportunities that bring prosperity into my life."

Growth Work for Home Play:

Opportunity List:
Write down 3 opportunities you have overlooked in the past—whether they were job offers, personal relationships, or financial opportunities. Reflect on how you can become more open to future opportunities and learn from the ones you missed.

Opportunity Awareness:
For the next week, keep an "opportunity journal." Each day, write down any opportunities you notice, no matter how small. It could be a chance to connect with someone new, a creative idea, or an unexpected offer. Pay attention to how being more aware of opportunities changes your perspective.

Discussion Points:

1. What opportunities have you overlooked because you were too focused on scarcity or fear?
2. How can you open yourself up to opportunities without letting fear dictate your decisions?

As I walked home, I felt lighter, as if the world around me had expanded. The fox's wisdom had shown me that opportunities were not something distant or unreachable—they were here, all around me, waiting for me to open my eyes and seize them. With each step, I felt more confident, more ready to welcome the abundance that life had to offer.

Hare whispered in my Dreams; Embracing Your Beauty and Uniqueness, the ideal spirit animal guide would be the Peacock. The peacock symbolizes self-expression, confidence, and embracing one's unique beauty without fear of judgment. With its vibrant and colorful feathers, the peacock reminds us to shine brightly and unapologetically, celebrating our individuality.

The peacock will guide you to embrace your inner and outer beauty, your talents, and your unique qualities that set you apart. It teaches that true prosperity comes from owning your uniqueness and letting it be seen by the world, just as the peacock proudly displays its feathers for all to admire.

Chapter 8:

The Peacock's Elegance – Embracing Your Beauty and Uniqueness

The day was warm, and a soft breeze whispered through the trees as I sat beneath my oak, preparing for another shamanic journey. Today, I felt a stirring deep within me—an unease I hadn't fully recognized until now. I had always found it difficult to embrace the things that made me unique, to truly acknowledge my own beauty, both inside and out. Too often, I had hidden myself, afraid of being seen, afraid that if I stood out, I might not be accepted.

But now, I was ready to confront this. I had learned about the power of choice, the flow of money as energy, and the importance of seeing opportunities. But what good were all these lessons if I couldn't accept and embrace my own uniqueness? I knew that in order to fully open myself to prosperity, I had to embrace who I was, in all my beauty and individuality.

Closing my eyes, I began to drift into the familiar mist of my inner world, the hare padding softly beside me as I moved deeper into the journey. But today, I was seeking another guide—one who could teach me the importance of owning my beauty and my uniqueness, one who could show me how to stand tall and proud in my true self.

As the mist cleared, I found myself standing in a lush, vibrant garden. The air was fragrant with the scent of blooming flowers, and in the distance, I saw a figure moving gracefully among the foliage. My heart quickened, knowing my guide awaited me.

From behind a large, flowering tree, a magnificent peacock emerged. Its feathers fanned out in an extravagant display of color—rich blues, greens, and golds shimmering in the sunlight. The peacock moved with a regal elegance, every step deliberate, its head held high, as if it were fully aware of its beauty and proud to show it. The hare sat beside me, watching quietly, as if encouraging me to approach.

The peacock, with its graceful movements, circled around me before finally stopping in front of me, its feathers shimmering with a brilliance that took my breath away.

"You seek to embrace your uniqueness," the peacock said, its voice soft but full of confidence. "You have spent too long hiding, believing that your beauty, your gifts, are something to be kept hidden. But it is time to let yourself be seen."

The peacock's words struck a chord deep within me. It was true. I had been hiding parts of myself for so long, afraid that if I allowed others to see my true self, I might be judged or rejected. But as I looked at the peacock, standing tall and unashamed in its magnificence, I realized that the only one holding me back was me.

"In what ways have you rejected your uniqueness or beauty?" the peacock asked, its eyes locking onto mine with an intensity that made me pause.

I closed my eyes and let the memories surface. I thought about the times I had downplayed my talents, not wanting to stand out too much. I remembered the moments when I had criticized my appearance, picking apart the things I didn't like about myself instead of celebrating what made me unique. I had told myself that blending in was safer, that being different was risky. And in doing so, I had dimmed my own light.

"I've hidden so much of who I am," I admitted, my voice trembling with the weight of the realization. "I've been afraid to fully embrace my uniqueness, afraid that I wouldn't be accepted if I stood out."

The peacock tilted its head slightly, as if considering my words. "And how has that served you?" it asked, its gaze never wavering.

I thought about it. How had it served me? Hiding hadn't brought me peace or fulfillment. If anything, it had blocked me from receiving the prosperity and joy I craved. By rejecting my own beauty and uniqueness, I had closed myself off from the abundance that could have flowed into my life.

"It hasn't served me," I said, my voice stronger now. "It's only held me back."

The peacock's feathers shimmered in the sunlight, and it took a step closer. "When you reject your uniqueness, you block prosperity," it said gently. "But when you embrace who you are—your beauty, your talents, and your individuality—you open the door to receiving all that life has to offer. Your uniqueness is your gift, and it is through this gift that abundance flows."

The truth of the peacock's words settled deep within me. I had been blocking my own prosperity by refusing to embrace the very things that made me special. The more I tried to hide, the more I distanced myself from the opportunities and abundance that were meant for me.

"How does embracing your true self lead to more abundance?" the peacock asked, its voice soft yet powerful.

I realized then that when I embraced my true self, I was stepping into alignment with my purpose. When I allowed myself to be seen, without fear or shame, I created space for abundance to flow into my life. Prosperity wasn't just about money—it was about being fully open to receiving love, joy, opportunities, and all the beauty that life had to offer. And that could only happen when I stopped hiding.

"Embracing my uniqueness allows me to receive," I said, my voice filled with new understanding. "It allows me to attract the prosperity that is meant for me."

The peacock nodded, its feathers shimmering with approval. "Exactly. You are meant to shine, to stand tall in your beauty. The world needs what you have to offer, but first, you must believe in your own worth. When you do, abundance will follow."

The peacock turned slightly, allowing its brilliant feathers to catch the light, as if to show me what it meant to fully embrace one's uniqueness. There was no fear, no hesitation—only pure, radiant confidence.

"Begin by acknowledging your beauty," the peacock said. "Every day, practice speaking kindly to yourself. Stand in front of the mirror and remind yourself of your worth. Tell yourself that you are beautiful, that you are unique, and that you are worthy of all the prosperity life has to offer."

I nodded, committing to the practice. It was time to stop hiding. It was time to embrace the beauty and uniqueness that had always been there, waiting to be acknowledged. I could feel the weight lifting from my shoulders as I realized that the only thing holding me back from prosperity had been my own self-judgment.

"And remember," the peacock said, its voice soft but filled with wisdom, "prosperity flows to those who are willing to be seen, who are willing to embrace their true selves without fear. When you shine, the world responds."

With that, the peacock turned and began to move gracefully back into the garden, its feathers trailing behind it like a cascade of color and light. The hare, who had been watching quietly, stepped forward, its eyes filled with understanding.

"Your beauty and uniqueness are your gifts," the hare said gently. "When you embrace them, you invite abundance into your life. Let yourself be seen."

I smiled, feeling a sense of peace and confidence rising within me. I whispered the affirmation aloud, sealing the lesson into my heart:

Affirmation:
"I embrace my beauty, my uniqueness, and my elegance as I attract prosperity."

Growth Work for Home Play:

Self-Reflection:

1. Write about "how embracing your uniqueness could create more prosperity in your life?".
2. Reflect on the ways in which you've hidden your gifts or rejected your beauty, and how stepping into your true self could open the door to abundance.

Daily Practice:

Each day, practice saying something kind to yourself in front of the mirror. Speak words of affirmation that reinforce your self-worth and beauty. Remind yourself that you are unique, and that your uniqueness is what attracts prosperity into your life.

Discussion Points:

1. In what ways have you rejected your uniqueness or beauty?
2. How does embracing your true self lead to more abundance?

As I stood and walked back home, I felt lighter, as though a part of me had been set free. With the wisdom of the peacock guiding me, I knew that embracing my beauty and uniqueness was the key to unlocking the prosperity I had been seeking. I was ready to shine, ready to be seen, and ready to receive all the abundance that was meant for me.

Hare whispered in my Dreams; Expanding Your Reach, the ideal spirit animal guide would be the Spider. The spider represents creativity, patience, and interconnectedness. Known for weaving intricate webs, the spider teaches us how everything is connected and how to expand our influence and reach by building networks, both seen and unseen. The spider's wisdom can help you understand the power of connection, communication, and expanding your reach through intentional actions, much like how a spider carefully crafts its web to capture what it needs.

In this chapter, the spider will guide you to expand your reach in life, business, and relationships, showing you how to patiently and skillfully weave the connections that will bring abundance and opportunity into your life.

Chapter 9: The Spider's Web – Expanding Your Reach

The air was still, with a hint of mystery as I stood beneath my usual oak tree, ready to embark on another shamanic journey. My heart felt heavy with a desire for growth. I had learned so much about abundance, energy, and embracing my true self, but there was something I had yet to master: expanding my reach. I knew that prosperity wasn't just about receiving—it was about sharing, connecting, and allowing myself to be seen by the world. But how could I expand my influence? How could I reach more people and allow more opportunities into my life?

With these thoughts swirling in my mind, I closed my eyes and allowed myself to drift into the familiar mist of my inner world. I felt the hare, as always, quietly padding alongside me, guiding me to the next spirit who would teach me how to extend my reach, just as the web of life connects everything around us.

As the mist lifted, I found myself in a lush, dense forest. It was alive with the sounds of life—the rustling of leaves, the chirping of birds, and the soft hum of insects. In the heart of the forest, I saw it—a delicate, intricate web stretched between two trees, shimmering in the soft glow of the sunlight filtering through the canopy. I moved closer, mesmerized by the complexity and beauty of the web. Every strand was perfectly woven, each connection leading to another, creating a vast network that seemed to hum with energy.

And then, from the shadows, a spider appeared. It moved gracefully along the strands of its web, its legs gliding effortlessly over the delicate threads. The spider's movements were both purposeful and fluid, as if it knew exactly how to navigate the web it had created.

The spider, sensing my presence, stopped and turned toward me. Its eyes glistened with wisdom, and though small, it radiated a sense of quiet power.

"You have come to learn how to expand your reach," the spider said, its voice soft yet filled with meaning. "You are like the web I weave. Every action, every connection you make, creates a new thread that can reach out into the world, touching others and drawing prosperity into your life."

I stood there, taking in the beauty of the spider's web, realizing the profound lesson it carried. Just as the spider weaves its web to capture what it needs, I too could create connections that would allow more opportunities, people, and abundance into my life. But first, I needed to learn how to weave those threads, how to expand beyond the limitations I had set for myself.

"How have you limited yourself in reaching out to others?" the spider asked, its voice curious and knowing.

I paused, reflecting on the question. I had always been hesitant to reach out, to share my gifts with others. Whether it was fear of rejection or a belief that my voice wasn't needed, I had often held myself back. I had told myself that it was safer to stay small, to keep my circle tight, rather than extending myself into the unknown. But now, as I stood before the spider, I realized how these limitations had prevented me from expanding my reach—and in doing so, had blocked my prosperity.

"I've limited myself out of fear," I admitted, my voice quiet but steady. "I've been afraid to share my gifts with the world, afraid of what might happen if I reach too far."

The spider moved closer, its delicate legs gliding across the web. "Fear creates small webs," it said softly. "But you are capable of weaving something much larger, much more intricate. Every thread you weave is an opportunity to connect with others, to share your gifts, and to allow prosperity to flow into your life."

I felt a surge of understanding wash over me. The spider was right. I had been keeping my web small, afraid to extend myself into new territories, afraid to make connections that could lead to greater opportunities.

"How does expanding your reach open you to more prosperity?" the spider asked, its voice a gentle reminder that I already knew the answer.

I thought about it. When I allowed myself to reach out, to connect with others, I wasn't just opening myself up to new relationships—I was opening myself up to new possibilities, new ideas, new paths that could lead to abundance. Every connection I made was a thread in my web, and the more threads I wove, the stronger my web would become.

"When I reach out, I create more opportunities for abundance to flow into my life," I said, my voice filled with newfound confidence. "Every connection expands my reach, and with it, my prosperity."

The spider nodded, its eyes gleaming with approval. "Exactly. You are not meant to keep your gifts hidden. You are meant to share them, to weave a web that connects you to the world. When you expand your reach, you expand your ability to receive."

The spider paused for a moment, then spoke again. "Begin by creating an action plan," it said. "Think of ways you can expand your reach, whether in your personal life or your business. Write down the steps you will take to connect with more people, and then, take action."

I nodded, understanding the importance of putting my intentions into practice. It wasn't enough to simply want to expand my reach—I needed to actively take steps toward it.

"And," the spider continued, "challenge yourself to reach out to three new people this week. Whether for personal or professional growth, make those connections. Each one is a thread in your web, and with each new thread, you strengthen your reach."

I smiled, feeling a sense of excitement rise within me. This was a challenge I was ready to embrace. I could already think of people I wanted to reach out to, connections I had been hesitant to make but now felt empowered to pursue.

The spider, sensing my readiness, moved back to its web, continuing to weave with a quiet grace. The hare, who had been watching from the sidelines, stepped forward, its eyes filled with warmth.

"Your web is yours to weave," the hare said softly. "With each new connection, you expand your reach, and with it, your prosperity. Trust in your ability to create the web that will bring abundance into your life."

I nodded, feeling a deep sense of clarity and purpose. I whispered the affirmation aloud, sealing the lesson into my heart:

Affirmation:
"I am open to reaching more people and sharing my gifts with the world."

Growth Work for Home Play:

Action Plan:

Create a plan to expand your reach, whether in your personal life, career, or business. Write down specific steps you will take to connect with more people, whether through social media, personal interactions, or networking opportunities.

Growth Challenge:

- Challenge yourself to reach out to three new people this week. This could be for personal growth, professional networking, or simply to create new connections.
- Reflect on how expanding your reach opens you up to new opportunities for prosperity.

Discussion Points:

1. How have you limited yourself in reaching out to others?
2. How does expanding your reach open you to more prosperity?

As I walked back from my journey, the image of the spider's web lingered in my mind. I could feel the threads of my own web beginning to take shape—each one representing a new connection, a new opportunity. The spider had shown me the power of reaching out, of weaving a web that extended far beyond what I had imagined. With each new step, I knew I was expanding my reach, and with it, my capacity to receive all the abundance life had to offer.

Hare whispered in my Dreams; Embracing Money with Joy, the ideal spirit animal guide would be the Hummingbird. The hummingbird represents joy, lightness, and the ability to move swiftly and freely between opportunities, much like how energy, including money, flows in and out of our lives. It symbolizes resilience, adaptability, and finding the sweetness in life, just as we must learn to see money not as something heavy or scarce, but as energy that flows effortlessly when we align with it.

The hummingbird will guide you in understanding the Joy of money's energy and how to embrace its flow without fear or restriction, much like how the hummingbird moves from flower to flower, effortlessly drawing in the nectar.

Chapter 10:

The Hummingbird's Dance – Embracing Money as Joy

The sun was high in the sky, casting a golden glow over the landscape as I sat beneath my oak tree, preparing for my next shamanic journey. This time, I was ready to explore a concept that had eluded me for most of my life—money as energy. Money had always felt like something solid and heavy, something to be earned, controlled, and carefully managed. But what if it wasn't? What if money was simply energy, neutral and abundant, waiting to flow into my life if only I allowed it?

With that thought, I closed my eyes and felt myself slip into the misty world of my inner journey. The familiar presence of the hare was beside me, soft and comforting, guiding me through the swirling fog. But today, I was searching for a new guide—one who could teach me how to embrace the lightness and flow of money's energy, one who could show me that abundance was already all around me, waiting to be welcomed.

As the mist cleared, I found myself standing in a bright, vibrant meadow. Flowers of every color dotted the landscape, swaying gently in the breeze. And then I saw it—a flash of iridescent green darting between the flowers, moving so swiftly that it was almost impossible to follow. It was a hummingbird.

The tiny creature zipped from bloom to bloom, its wings beating so fast they seemed to blur. Yet, despite its speed, the hummingbird exuded a sense of grace and joy. It was small, but powerful, and every movement it made seemed effortless.

The hare nudged me gently, and I knew the hummingbird was the guide I had come to meet. Its lightness, its speed, and its ability to draw nectar from the flowers so effortlessly were exactly what I needed to understand about the flow of money—how it could be light, joyful, and abundant if only I allowed it to be.

The hummingbird hovered in front of me, its wings creating a soft hum that filled the air with a sense of energy and life. Its eyes met mine, and I felt a sense of connection, as if this tiny creature understood the questions I carried in my heart.

"You have come to learn about money as energy," the hummingbird said, its voice light but filled with wisdom. "Money is not something heavy or scarce. It is energy—neutral, positive, and abundant. It flows, much like the wind beneath my wings, and it will flow into your life with ease if you treat it with love and gratitude."

I felt a wave of understanding wash over me. The hummingbird's words were simple, yet profound. I had spent so much time viewing money as something to be controlled, something that required effort and struggle. But now, as I watched the hummingbird dance through the air, I realized that money, like any form of energy, could be light, fluid, and joyful.

"How does viewing money as energy shift your relationship with it?" the hummingbird asked, hovering gracefully in front of me.

I paused, reflecting on the question. How would my relationship with money change if I saw it as energy rather than something solid or scarce? I realized that I would no longer fear money or feel anxious about it. Instead of seeing it as something I needed to hold tightly or manage, I could begin to trust that money, like energy, would flow into my life when I was aligned with it.

"It would change everything," I said slowly, feeling the truth of my words. "I wouldn't feel the need to control money so tightly. I could allow it to flow, trusting that it would come and go naturally, just as energy does."

The hummingbird's wings hummed softly, and it nodded. "Exactly. Money, like all energy, responds to how you treat it. When you hold it with love, respect, and gratitude, it flows to you effortlessly. But when you treat it with fear, judgment, or anxiety, you block its flow."

The hummingbird hovered closer, its tiny body shimmering in the sunlight. "Now," it said gently, "take out a physical coin or bill. Hold it in your hand, and feel its energy. Do not judge it, but simply feel the life force it carries. Money, like all things, is energy. And it can bring you joy if you allow it to flow freely."

I reached into my pocket and pulled out a small coin, holding it carefully in my palm. As I closed my eyes and focused on the object, I allowed myself to feel its energy. It was light, almost buzzing with potential. For the first time, I realized that money wasn't something to be feared or judged—it was just another form of energy, waiting to be engaged with.

"How does it feel?" the hummingbird asked, its voice soft.

"It feels... neutral," I said, surprised by the simplicity of the sensation. "It doesn't carry any of the weight I've always associated with it. It's just energy."

The hummingbird fluttered its wings joyfully, and I could sense its approval. "That is the truth of money. It is neither good nor bad—it is simply energy. When you welcome it into your life with Joy and gratitude, it will flow to you naturally."

I smiled, feeling a sense of lightness filling my heart. I understood now that my relationship with money didn't have to be one of fear or control. Instead, it could be one of ease, trust, and gratitude.

"How can gratitude for money create more abundance?" the hummingbird asked, its eyes filled with wisdom.

I thought about it. Gratitude was a powerful force—it opened the heart and allowed more of what we were thankful for to flow into our lives. If I could approach money with gratitude, instead of fear or scarcity, I could create space for more of it to enter my reality.

"Gratitude makes room for more abundance," I said softly. "When I'm thankful for the money I have, I invite more of it into my life."

The hummingbird's eyes sparkled, and it flitted from flower to flower with an almost playful energy. "Exactly. When you are grateful for money, you are acknowledging its energy, and that gratitude creates a magnet for more. Every time you handle money, say 'thank you.' Treat it with respect and love, and it will return to you."

I nodded, committing to the practice. From now on, I would treat money with the same lightness and gratitude that the hummingbird embodied. Every time I handled money, whether it was paying a bill, receiving a payment, or making a purchase, I would say "thank you" and honor the energy it carried.

"Remember," the hummingbird said as it hovered in front of me, "money comes with Joy and like all energy, it flows where it is welcomed. Treat it with love, ease, and gratitude, and it will flow into your life abundantly."

With that, the hummingbird zoomed off, disappearing into the vibrant landscape as quickly as it had appeared. The hare, who had been quietly watching, stepped forward, its eyes filled with understanding.

"Money is not meant to be feared," the hare said softly. "It is a gift, an energy that flows through your life. When you embrace it with gratitude, you open yourself to receiving all the abundance that is meant for you."

I smiled, feeling a sense of peace and clarity wash over me. I whispered the affirmation aloud, sealing the lesson into my heart:

Affirmation:
"I welcome money into my life with love, ease, and gratitude."

Growth Work for Home Play:

Energy Exercise:

Take a physical bill or coin, and hold it in your hand. Close your eyes and focus on the energy it carries. Try not to judge it, but simply feel its presence with Joy. Reflect on how this energy feels and how you can engage with it more positively.

Gratitude Practice:

Each time you handle money this week—whether it's paying a bill, making a purchase, or receiving income—take a moment to say "thank you." This simple practice of gratitude will help you shift your mindset and open yourself up to receiving more abundance.

Discussion Points:

1. How does viewing money as energy shift your relationship with it?
2. How can Joy & gratitude for money create more abundance?

As I returned from my journey, I felt lighter, as if a weight had been lifted from my relationship with money. The hummingbird had taught me that money wasn't something to be controlled or feared—it was energy, neutral and abundant, waiting to flow into my life. And now, with each step I took, I knew I was opening myself to receive that energy with love, ease, and gratitude.

Hare whispered in my Dreams; Recognizing Your Value, the ideal spirit animal guide would be the Lion. The lion represents strength, courage, and self-confidence. It is a symbol of personal power and leadership, reminding you to recognize your own worth and stand tall in it. The lion teaches you to honor your value, not just in terms of what you can achieve, but in who you are intrinsically. It encourages you to step into your full potential with confidence and grace, knowing that your presence has immense value.

The lion will guide you to acknowledge your inner strength, helping you understand that recognizing your value is key to attracting prosperity and abundance.

Chapter 11:

The Lion's Roar – Recognizing Your Value

The afternoon sun was warm as I sat beneath the oak tree, the familiar grounding spot where my shamanic journeys always began. Today, my heart felt heavy with a question I had been carrying for some time: What is my true value?

For much of my life, I had measured my worth based on my financial success. My self-esteem had often risen and fallen with the amount of money in my bank account. But I knew, deep down, that my value had to be more than just a number. There was a part of me that longed to recognize my worth beyond money—to see my value in my talents, my presence, and the contributions I made to the world. But how could I unlock that understanding?

I closed my eyes and let myself drift into the familiar mist of my inner world, the hare once again guiding me through the swirling clouds. Today, though, I knew I needed a guide who could show me the strength that comes with recognizing my true value. I needed a guide who embodied power, confidence, and an unshakeable sense of worth.

As the mist cleared, I found myself standing in a vast savannah, the golden grass swaying gently in the breeze. In the distance, I saw a powerful figure—a creature that moved with the quiet authority of one who knew its worth. It was a lion.

The lion was magnificent, its golden mane flowing around its regal face. It walked with an effortless grace, exuding confidence in every step. The hare, always by my side, remained quietly watchful, allowing me to approach this new guide who could teach me what it meant to truly recognize my value.

The lion stopped and turned to face me, its amber eyes piercing yet calm. It stood tall and proud, as though it had nothing to prove. And in that moment, I understood—I was in the presence of an animal that knew its worth, an animal that embodied strength and self-respect. The lion didn't need to roar to assert its power; its mere presence was enough.

"You have come to recognize your value," the lion said, its voice deep and steady, much like the rumble of distant thunder. "But you have been limiting your worth to something external—something that can be measured and counted. You believe your value lies in money, but that is only a fraction of who you are."

The lion's words resonated deeply within me. It was true. I had always tied my sense of self-worth to my financial achievements. If I wasn't making enough money, I felt less valuable. But now, standing in the presence of the lion, I could see how narrow that belief was. My value wasn't just about what I earned—it was about who I was.

"In what ways do you currently measure your value?" the lion asked, its amber eyes fixed on mine.

I lowered my gaze, feeling a wave of vulnerability wash over me. I had always measured my value by external achievements—by how much money I made, by the recognition I received, by the things I owned. But those things, I now realized, didn't truly define me. They were temporary, fleeting. I needed to see my value beyond those metrics.

"I've measured my value by money," I admitted softly, "by what I can achieve, and by how others perceive me."

The lion tilted its head slightly, as if considering my words. "And how has that served you?"

I thought about it. My constant focus on external validation had left me feeling empty at times, always chasing more, but never feeling fulfilled. Even when I achieved financial success, it didn't last. There was always a sense that I wasn't enough, that I needed to do more to prove my worth.

"It hasn't served me," I said, my voice stronger now. "I've been chasing something that can never truly define me."

The lion nodded, its mane shimmering in the sunlight. "Your value," it said, "comes from within. It is in your unique gifts, your presence, your heart. Money is simply one reflection of your energy, but it does not define you. When you recognize your value beyond money, you open yourself to receiving true prosperity in all forms."

The lion's words were like a key unlocking a door inside me. I could see now that my worth was not tied to my bank account. My value was in who I was—in my kindness, my creativity, my ability to connect with others, and the way I showed up in the world.

"How would your reality shift if you recognized your value beyond financial terms?" the lion asked, its voice filled with gentle wisdom.

I thought about it. If I could truly embrace my value beyond money, I would no longer feel the constant pressure to prove myself through external means. I would feel lighter, freer. I would know that I was worthy of love, respect, and abundance simply because of who I was—not because of what I could achieve or earn.

"It would change everything," I said softly, a smile forming on my lips. "I would no longer chase after validation. I would trust in my own worth."

The lion's eyes softened, and it took a step closer. "Exactly. Your value is inherent. It cannot be taken away or diminished. When you embrace your worth, you attract prosperity naturally, because you are no longer looking for something outside of yourself to define you."

The lion's presence was powerful, but it wasn't intimidating. It was as if the lion knew that true strength came from within—and that recognizing your own value was the key to unlocking that strength.

"Begin by acknowledging your value every day," the lion said. "Stand in front of the mirror and affirm your worth. Say to yourself, 'I am valuable just as I am.' And mean it. Your value does not come from what you do—it comes from who you are."

I nodded, feeling a deep sense of clarity and peace. I knew now that my value wasn't something I had to earn or prove. It was something I already possessed. The lion had shown me the way to reclaim that understanding.

"Write about how your value enriches your life and the lives of others," the lion continued. "Reflect on the ways you contribute to the world beyond money. Your value is in your presence, your talents, your kindness. It is in the way you show up for yourself and for others."

I smiled, grateful for the lion's wisdom. I could see now how recognizing my true value would open me to more abundance—not just in terms of money, but in love, joy, and fulfillment. By embracing my worth, I would no longer block the flow of prosperity into my life.

"Remember," the lion said, its voice soft but strong, "your value is infinite. When you recognize it, you step into your true power. And when you stand in your power, the world responds."

The lion's golden mane shimmered in the sunlight as it turned to walk back into the savannah. The hare, always present, stepped forward, its eyes filled with quiet understanding.

"You are valuable," the hare said gently. "And when you recognize your worth, you invite prosperity into your life in ways you never imagined."

I stood tall, feeling a sense of empowerment rise within me. I whispered the affirmation aloud, sealing it into my heart:

Affirmation:
"I recognize my worth beyond just money and open myself to the value I offer."

Growth Work for Home Play:

Value Recognition:

Write about how your value enriches your life and the lives of others, independent of money. Reflect on the ways you contribute to the world, through your talents, your kindness, your presence, and your heart.

Daily Mirror Work

Each morning, stand in front of the mirror and affirm your value with a positive statement. Say, "I am valuable just as I am," and allow yourself to believe it. This daily practice will help you internalize your worth, independent of external achievements.

Discussion Points:

1. In what ways do you currently measure your value?
2. How would your reality shift if you recognized your value beyond financial terms?

As I walked back from my journey, I felt a new sense of strength and confidence within me. The lion had taught me that my value was not something I had to earn—it was something I already had. And by recognizing that, I knew I was opening myself to receive all the prosperity, joy, and abundance that life had to offer.

Hare whispered in my Dreams; Embracing Support and Opportunities, the ideal spirit animal guide would be the Dolphin. Dolphins are known for their intelligence, playfulness, and strong social bonds. They symbolize collaboration, communication, and the ability to navigate through life's currents with joy and ease. Dolphins are highly social creatures, thriving in communities and supporting one another, which makes them perfect guides for learning to embrace support and recognize opportunities.

The dolphin will teach you how to open up to support from others, trust in collaboration, and see the opportunities that come through connection and teamwork.

Chapter 12:

The Dolphin's Wisdom – Embracing Support and Opportunities

The sound of ocean waves filled my senses as I sat beneath the familiar oak tree, ready to embark on another journey. Today, I felt a deep sense of curiosity. I had spent much of my life believing I needed to do everything on my own—rejecting help, resisting collaboration, and missing out on opportunities because of fear or pride. But now, I was ready to learn the art of receiving support and embracing the opportunities that life offers.

I closed my eyes and let myself drift into the swirling mist of my shamanic journey. As always, the hare was beside me, its presence a comforting reminder that I was never truly alone on this path. But today, I was seeking guidance from a creature that could show me how to move through life with ease, joy, and openness—how to swim with the currents of life rather than against them.

As the mist cleared, I found myself standing on the shore of a vast, shimmering ocean. The water was a brilliant blue, reflecting the sunlight in sparkles of light. It was peaceful, but I could sense something more—a presence just beneath the surface, waiting to guide me.

Suddenly, I saw it—a sleek and graceful dolphin leaping joyfully from the water, its body glistening in the sunlight. It moved with such ease, its playful energy radiating a sense of freedom and connection. The hare stood quietly beside me as the dolphin swam closer, its movements smooth and confident.

The dolphin surfaced, its eyes meeting mine with a playful intelligence. I could feel its energy—light, free, and unburdened by the fears and doubts that had often held me back. This was a creature that knew how to embrace the flow of life, how to move with the currents and trust in the support of its community. I knew immediately that dolphin would teach me how to open myself to the opportunities and support I resisted.

"You seek to embrace support and opportunities," the dolphin said, its voice filled with warmth and joy. "Haven't you been swimming against the currents, rejecting the very things that could bring you more prosperity."

The dolphin's words struck a chord deep within me. It was true. I had rejected opportunities out of fear—fear that I wasn't ready, fear that I might fail, or simply fear of change. But now, as I watched the dolphin effortlessly glide through the water, I realized how much I had been missing by trying to go it alone.

"Reflect on the times when you rejected support or opportunities," the dolphin said, its eyes twinkling with knowing. "Why did you turn them down?"

I closed my eyes and let the memories come to the surface. I thought about the job offers I had declined because I was afraid of stepping outside my comfort zone. I remembered the times when friends or colleagues had offered help, I had often turned down help from them, determined to prove and Convinced that I could handle everything on my own. I had always believed that accepting help was a sign of weakness, but now I could see how that belief had held me back from greater abundance.

"I've rejected help out of fear and pride," I admitted, my voice soft. "I didn't want to seem weak or incapable. And sometimes, I was just too afraid to say yes to new opportunities."

The dolphin let out a soft, playful sound, almost like a chuckle. "You are not alone in this," it said gently. "Many people reject support because they believe they must carry everything on their own. But true strength comes from knowing when to accept help. And opportunities are gifts—they are the universe's way of offering you new paths to prosperity. When you reject them, you close yourself off from the flow of abundance."

The dolphin's words washed over me like a wave of clarity. I had always believed that saying yes to help would make me seem less capable, but now I realized that it was quite the opposite. Accepting support didn't make me weak—it made me wise. And by opening myself up, I was inviting prosperity into my life.

"How can embracing support from others lead to more prosperity?" the dolphin asked, its eyes sparkling as it dove back into the water, surfacing a moment later with a playful splash.

I thought about it. When I accepted support from others—whether emotional, financial, or practical—I was allowing myself to be part of a greater flow of energy. Support didn't mean losing control; it meant working with others to create something greater than I could achieve alone. By embracing opportunities, I wasn't giving up my independence—I was expanding my reach, allowing new possibilities to enter my life.

"Embracing support creates space for more abundance," I said, my voice filled with new understanding. "It allows me to grow, to expand, and to invite more opportunities into my life."

The dolphin leaped out of the water again, its movements graceful and effortless. "Exactly," it said. "Prosperity flows where there is openness. When you are willing to say yes—to help, to opportunities, to support—you are aligning yourself with the natural currents of life. And life, much like the ocean, is always offering you new ways to grow and thrive."

The dolphin swam in circles, creating ripples in the water that seemed to radiate outwards, touching everything around them. I realized then that opportunities and support were like those ripples—once I allowed them into my life, they would spread, creating new paths and connections that would lead to even greater prosperity.

"Begin by keeping an opportunity journal," the dolphin said, its eyes gleaming with wisdom. "Reflect on three opportunities or offers of support that you recently rejected. Write down why you turned them down, and consider what might have changed if you had accepted them."

I nodded, knowing this exercise would help me understand how my resistance to support had limited me. By acknowledging the opportunities I had missed, I could begin to shift my mindset and embrace the ones that were yet to come.

"And for the next week," the dolphin continued, "commit to saying yes to new opportunities and support when they arise. Challenge yourself to be open, even if it feels uncomfortable at first. The more you practice saying yes, the more you will open yourself to the flow of prosperity."

I smiled, feeling a sense of excitement bubbling up within me. This was a challenge I was ready to accept. I could already see how saying yes to support and opportunities would create more ease and abundance in my life.

The dolphin swam closer, its eyes filled with kindness. "Remember," it said softly, "you are never alone. The universe is always offering you help, in many forms. When you embrace that support, you allow yourself to grow, to thrive, and to prosper."

With that, the dolphin leaped joyfully into the air one last time before diving back into the depths of the ocean. The hare, always by my side, looked up at me, its eyes filled with understanding.

"You don't have to do it all on your own," the hare said gently. "Embrace the support that is offered to you, and let the opportunities flow into your life."

I stood on the shore, feeling the weight of my old fears lift away. I whispered the affirmation aloud, letting it anchor itself in my heart:

Affirmation:
"I am open to receiving opportunities and support in all forms."

Growth Work for Home Play:

Opportunity Journal:

Reflect on three opportunities or offers of support that you recently rejected. Write down why you rejected them and what might have changed if you had accepted them. This reflection will help you understand how your resistance to support may have limited your growth.

Openness Challenge:

For the next week, commit to saying "yes" to new opportunities and support when they arise. Whether it's help from a friend, a new job offer, or simply an idea that sparks something within you, practice being open to what comes your way.

Notice how this openness creates more ease and flow in your life.

Discussion Points:

1. Reflect on times when you rejected support or opportunities. Why did you turn them down?
2. How can embracing support from others lead to more prosperity?

As I returned from my journey, I felt a sense of lightness and freedom. The dolphin had shown me that embracing support and opportunities wasn't a sign of weakness—it was a path to greater abundance. By saying yes, I was allowing the natural flow of life to guide me toward more prosperity, more joy, and more connection. And with each step, I knew I was no longer swimming against the currents, but moving with them, open and ready to receive all that life had to offer.

Hare whispered in my Dreams; For the Purpose of Money, the ideal spirit animal guide would be the Buffalo. The buffalo symbolizes abundance, gratitude, and the recognition of resources as sacred. It represents the balance between material wealth and spiritual abundance, reminding us that money is a tool, not the end goal. The buffalo teaches us to honour the energy of money, to use it wisely, and to understand its deeper purpose in supporting our life's journey and the collective good.

The buffalo will guide you to see money as a resource meant to be respected and used to create prosperity. It will also remind you to remain grounded and connected to the true purpose behind wealth.

Chapter 13:

The Buffalo's Wisdom – The Purpose of Money

The sky stretched wide and open, the sun setting in a brilliant display of reds and golds as I sat beneath my oak tree, ready for another journey. This time, my thoughts were centered on money, but not in the usual way. I had spent much of my life seeing money as something stressful—something to chase, manage, and worry over. But recently, I had begun to wonder: What if money wasn't the source of stress, but rather a tool for creation, joy, and freedom?

With that question in mind, I closed my eyes, allowing myself to slip into the familiar mist of my shamanic journey. As always, the hare was there, guiding me through the swirling fog. But today, I knew my guide would be different. I was seeking an animal that could show me the deeper purpose of money, an animal that could help me understand how to use money as a tool, not a source of anxiety.

As the mist cleared, I found myself standing in an expansive, golden plain. The earth beneath my feet felt solid, grounding, and I could feel the strength of the land itself. In the distance, I saw a powerful figure—a creature that moved slowly but with purpose, its presence commanding the entire landscape. It was a buffalo.

The buffalo's massive form was awe-inspiring. Its dark, shaggy coat rippled with strength, and yet there was a gentleness to its movements, as if it understood the balance between power and grace. The hare remained by my side, watching quietly as I approached this new guide who could teach me the true purpose of money.

The buffalo stood tall, its dark eyes calm and wise, and I felt a deep sense of respect for the creature before me. The buffalo, with its connection to the earth and its embodiment of abundance, seemed to carry the wisdom I was seeking.

"You have come to learn the purpose of money," the buffalo said, its voice deep and resonant, like the rumble of distant thunder. "But you must understand that money, like all resources, is a tool. It is not the goal itself."

The buffalo's words settled over me, and I immediately felt the weight of them. It was true. I had spent so long seeing money as the destination—as something to accumulate, to worry over, to chase. But now, standing before the buffalo, I realized how limited that perspective was. Money wasn't the end—it was simply a means to an end, a tool that could be used for joy, creation, and experiences that enriched life.

"How do you currently view the purpose of money?" the buffalo asked, its deep gaze fixed on me.

I hesitated, thinking about my past relationship with money. I had always seen it as something to manage carefully, something to stress over. My thoughts had been filled with concerns about having enough, earning enough, and saving enough. But what if money could be something more? What if it could be light, fun, and creative?

"I've always seen money as something to stress about," I admitted softly. "But I'm starting to understand that it could be a tool for creating joy."

The buffalo nodded, its massive head lowering slightly as if in approval. "Money is energy, like all things," it said. "Its purpose is not to be hoarded or feared, but to be used. When you see money as a tool, you open yourself to using it in ways that bring joy, creation, and abundance into your life. The more you respect its purpose, the more freely it will flow."

I felt a shift within me, as if a door had opened to a new understanding. The buffalo was right—money wasn't meant to be something heavy and burdensome. It was a resource, much like the earth beneath my feet, meant to support life, growth, and creation. When I treated money with respect, when I saw it as a tool rather than something to fear, I could begin to use it to enhance my life in meaningful ways.

"What would change in your life if you saw money as a tool for joy and creation rather than stress?" the buffalo asked, its voice gentle but filled with wisdom.

I closed my eyes and imagined what my life could look like if I embraced money as a tool for creation. I saw myself using it to invest in experiences that brought me joy—traveling, learning new skills, creating art. I saw myself sharing it with others, using it to support causes and people I cared about. And in this vision, money flowed freely. There was no stress, no fear, just a sense of lightness and ease.

"Everything would change," I said, my voice filled with new understanding. "I would no longer feel trapped by money. I would use it to create, to play, to live fully."

The buffalo's eyes softened, and it stepped closer, its presence calm and grounding. "Exactly. Money is a tool for play, creation, and joy in your life. When you treat it as such, you allow it to flow freely, and you invite more abundance into your life."

The buffalo's words resonated deeply with me. I could feel the truth of them sinking in. Money wasn't meant to be a source of stress—it was meant to be used, to create experiences that brought joy and fulfillment.

"Begin by playing with money," the buffalo said. "Write down how you can use money in ways that bring joy to yourself and others. Invest in experiences that uplift you, that make you feel alive. When you use money with this intention, you honor its purpose."

I nodded, feeling a sense of excitement. The buffalo had shown me a new way to engage with money—a way that felt joyful, creative, and light. I was ready to play with money, to use it as a tool for living fully, rather than something to fear or control.

"And this week," the buffalo continued, "take a small amount of money and spend it purely on something that brings you joy or helps you create something new. It doesn't have to be much—just enough to remind you that money is meant to serve your life, not control it."

I smiled, grateful for the buffalo's wisdom. I could already think of ways to use money in ways that felt joyful—perhaps a new book, a small adventure, or a gift for someone I cared about. The possibilities felt endless, and for the first time in a long time, money didn't feel heavy. It felt like a gift, a resource to be used wisely and joyfully.

The buffalo stepped back, its large form moving with a grace that belied its size. The hare, always by my side, nudged me gently, as if to remind me that this was a lesson I was ready to embody.

"Remember," the buffalo said, its voice filled with quiet strength, "money is a tool for creation, not a source of fear. Use it wisely, and it will serve you well. When you honor its purpose, it will flow into your life with ease."

I whispered the affirmation aloud, letting the lesson sink into my heart:

Affirmation:
"Money is a tool for play, creation, and joy in my life."

Growth Work for Home Play:

Play with Money:
Write down how you can begin using money in playful and joyful ways. This could be investing in fun experiences, sharing it with others, or using it to create something new. Reflect on how you can treat money as a tool for enhancing your life.

Creative Challenge:
Take a small amount of money this week and spend it purely on something that brings you joy or helps you create something new. Whether it's a personal treat, a creative project, or a shared experience, use money in a way that feels light and fun.

Discussion Points:

1. How do you currently view the purpose of money?
2. What would change in your life if you saw money as a tool for joy and creation rather than stress?

As I returned from my journey, I felt a deep sense of peace. The buffalo had shown me that money wasn't something to be feared or controlled—it was a tool, a resource that could be used to create joy, to play, to live fully. And with each step I took, I knew I was moving toward a new relationship with money—one that was rooted in respect, ease, and the joyful purpose it was meant to serve.

Hare whispered in my Dreams; Letting Go of Being 'Good' to Receive, the ideal spirit animal guide would be the Coyote. The coyote is often associated with wisdom through trickery and transformation, representing the idea that the pursuit of being "good" or conforming to societal expectations can sometimes limit personal growth and receiving abundance. The coyote teaches the importance of breaking free from rigid expectations, letting go of perfectionism, and embracing your authentic self to allow abundance into your life.

The coyote will guide you to shed the need to constantly be "good" or "perfect" and help you open yourself to receiving in unexpected and unconventional ways.

Chapter 14

The Coyote's Trick – Letting Go of Being 'Good' to Receive

The morning was still, the sky softly glowing with the first light of dawn as I sat beneath my oak tree. Today's journey felt different. There was a tension in my heart, a feeling I had been carrying for years: the belief that I had to earn abundance, that I had to be good enough to deserve it. It was a weight I had unknowingly placed on myself, believing that prosperity only flowed to those who were perfect or who followed every rule. But now, I was ready to release that belief, to let go of the need for approval, and to embrace receiving without judgment.

I closed my eyes and felt the familiar mist of my shamanic journey surround me. The hare, as always, was by my side, its quiet presence comforting me as we ventured into the unknown. But today, I was seeking a guide who could teach me how to break free from this self-imposed limitation—a guide who knew the power of trickery, transformation, and stepping outside the bounds of what is considered "good."

As the mist cleared, I found myself in a vast desert, the golden sands stretching out endlessly before me. The air was warm, and the sky above was a brilliant, cloudless blue. In the distance, I saw movement—a quick, agile figure darting between the rocks. It was a coyote.

The coyote moved with a playful energy, its body low to the ground as it zigzagged across the desert floor, stopping only to glance in my direction with knowing eyes. It was a creature of wisdom, but not the kind of wisdom that comes from following rules. This was the wisdom of breaking free, of questioning conventions, of learning to trust yourself and your instincts.

The hare nudged me gently, urging me forward, and I approached the coyote with a mixture of curiosity and hesitation. The coyote, sensing my uncertainty, let out a soft chuckle, its eyes gleaming with mischief.

"You've come to let go of being 'good' to receive," the coyote said, its voice filled with humor. "But you're still clinging to the belief that you must earn your place in the world, aren't you?"

I paused, feeling a wave of vulnerability wash over me. The coyote's words cut straight to the heart of the matter. I had spent so much of my life trying to be good, to be perfect, believing that only then would I be worthy of abundance. But the more I tried to meet these impossible standards, the more I felt like I was failing—and the further prosperity seemed to slip away from me.

"Yes," I admitted softly, my voice barely a whisper. "I've always believed I had to be good enough to deserve abundance."

The coyote let out another laugh, this one light and free. It darted around me in circles, its movements quick and unpredictable. "Who told you that you had to be 'good' to receive anything?" it asked, its eyes twinkling with mischief. "Who decided that abundance was something you had to earn?"

I thought about the question, feeling the weight of years of conditioning. Society, upbringing, expectations—all of these had taught me that I needed to work hard, follow the rules, and be perfect in order to be rewarded. But standing here in the presence of the coyote, I realized how limiting that belief had been.

"I don't know," I said, my voice a little stronger now. "I just thought that was how things worked."

The coyote stopped its playful dance and sat before me, its gaze suddenly serious. "Let me tell you something," it said, its voice low and steady. "The universe doesn't care if you're perfect. The universe doesn't require you to be good in order to receive. Abundance flows to those who are open to it—not to those who try to earn it through some impossible standard of goodness."

The coyote's words hit me like a wave of truth. I had spent so much of my life trying to be "good," trying to fit into a mold that wasn't even real. And in doing so, I had blocked myself from receiving. I had closed the door to abundance because I didn't believe I was worthy of it unless I was perfect.

"How does the need to be 'good' or perfect limit your ability to receive?" the coyote asked, its eyes watching me closely.

I took a deep breath and thought about it. My constant striving for perfection had left me feeling exhausted and unworthy. I had believed that I needed to earn every bit of prosperity that came my way, and if I didn't meet the standard, I told myself that I didn't deserve it. But now, I could see how flawed that thinking was. Abundance wasn't something I had to earn—it was something I could allow myself to receive.

"It limits me completely," I said quietly. "I've been so focused on being good that I've blocked myself from receiving. I didn't think I deserved abundance unless I was perfect."

The coyote nodded, its eyes softening. "And what would happen if you let go of that need? What would change if you allowed yourself to receive without judgment?"

I closed my eyes and imagined it—what it would feel like to receive abundance without guilt, without feeling like I had to earn it. It felt light, freeing. I could see myself enjoying life more, opening up to opportunities, and accepting the gifts that the universe had to offer without questioning whether I was worthy.

"I would be free," I whispered, a smile forming on my lips. "I would finally allow myself to receive without judgment."

The coyote let out another playful laugh, its eyes gleaming with approval. "Exactly. The moment you let go of the need to be 'good,' you open yourself to receiving all the abundance that's waiting for you. The universe isn't judging you—it's offering you gifts. All you have to do is say yes."

The coyote began to move again, darting around me with a newfound sense of joy. "Practice receiving without judgment," it said. "Reflect on how you might be limiting yourself because you feel you don't deserve abundance. And do something for yourself without guilt—something that brings you joy, simply because you can."

I nodded, feeling a surge of excitement. I was ready to release the need to be "good" and allow myself to receive freely. The coyote's playful energy was contagious, and I felt a lightness in my heart that I hadn't felt in years.

"Remember," the coyote said, its voice softening as it came to stand in front of me again, "you don't have to be perfect. You don't have to earn abundance. It's already yours—you just have to let yourself receive it."

With that, the coyote turned and ran off into the desert, its movements quick and free. The hare, always by my side, looked up at me, its eyes filled with understanding.

"You are worthy of receiving," the hare said gently. "Not because you are good, but because you are you."

I smiled, feeling a deep sense of peace settle over me. I whispered the affirmation aloud, letting the truth of it sink into my heart:

Affirmation:
"I release the need to be 'good' to receive abundance in all forms."

Growth Work for Home Play:

Receiving without Judgment:
Reflect on how you might limit yourself because you feel you don't deserve abundance. Write about the ways in which your need to be "good" has blocked you from receiving. Practice allowing yourself to receive without feeling the need to "earn" it.

Action Step:
This week, do something for yourself without guilt—something that you would normally feel you don't "deserve." Whether it's a small gift, a treat, or an experience, allow yourself to enjoy it without questioning your worthiness.

Discussion Points:

1. How does the need to be "good" or perfect limit your ability to receive?
2. How can releasing this need shift your relationship with abundance?

As I returned from my journey, I felt lighter, as if a burden I had been carrying for years had finally been lifted. The coyote had shown me that I didn't need to be perfect to receive. I didn't need to prove myself to anyone—not even to myself. And with each step I took, I knew I was opening myself to receive all the abundance that life had to offer, simply because I was ready to say yes.

Hare whispered in my Dreams; Showing Up and Committing, the ideal spirit animal guide would be the Horse. The horse represents strength, determination, and freedom through commitment. It symbolizes the power of showing up fully, taking decisive action, and committing to your path with passion and purpose. The horse teaches you to harness your energy and focus it toward achieving your goals, while also reminding you to stay grounded and connected to your inner strength.

The horse will guide you to show up fully in your life, commit to your goals, and stay steadfast on your path, even in the face of challenges. It encourages you to harness your inner power and move forward with confidence and dedication.

Chapter 15

The Horse's Strength – Showing Up and Committing

The wind swept across the open plains as I stood beneath my oak tree, feeling the stirrings of something powerful within me. I had spent much of my life dreaming, setting goals, and making plans, but somehow, I felt like I had been holding back. There were moments when I hesitated to fully commit—moments when I was present, but not fully engaged. Today, I was ready to change that. I was ready to learn how to show up fully for my life and commit to my path with the strength and determination it deserved.

With a deep breath, I closed my eyes and began my shamanic journey. The hare was with me, guiding me through the familiar mists of the spirit world. But this time, I felt the need for a guide that embodied strength, power, and the freedom that comes from unwavering commitment. I needed an animal that could teach me how to harness my inner energy, focus it, and show up fully for the life I wanted to create.

As the mist parted, I found myself standing in a vast, sunlit field. The ground beneath my feet was solid, yet open, stretching endlessly into the horizon. In the distance, I saw a majestic figure—a creature of grace and power, moving with an effortless sense of purpose. It was a horse.

The horse's muscles rippled under its sleek coat as it galloped across the field, its mane flowing in the wind. It was the embodiment of strength and commitment, moving forward with purpose and focus. The hare remained by my side, watching quietly as the horse approached, its eyes filled with wisdom and knowing.

As the horse came closer, it slowed to a graceful trot and then stopped just in front of me. Its presence was grounding yet invigorating, as if simply being near this powerful creature reminded me of the strength I already carried within me.

"You seek to learn how to show up fully for your life," the horse said, its voice deep and steady, like the rhythmic beat of hooves on the ground. "But you've been holding back, haven't you?"

I lowered my gaze, feeling the truth of the horse's words. It was true. There were moments in my life when I hesitated—when I avoided fully committing, whether out of fear or uncertainty. I had goals and dreams, but I hadn't always given them my all. And yet, here was this creature—this horse—standing before me, showing me what it meant to move forward with full commitment, with every step intentional and powerful.

"Yes," I admitted softly. "I've been holding back. I want to move forward, but sometimes I'm afraid of failing or unsure of the path."

The horse nodded, its eyes soft with understanding. "We all experience fear," it said, "but fear should not stop you from showing up. When you hold back, you deny yourself the opportunity to receive the abundance that life is offering you. Prosperity flows when you commit fully—when you harness your strength and move forward with purpose, even in the face of uncertainty."

The horse's words were like a spark of clarity. I could feel the truth that by holding back, I had limited myself, closing off opportunities for abundance and growth. But by showing up fully—by committing to my goals, my dreams, and my responsibilities—I could open the door to a life filled with prosperity.

"Where in your life are you holding back or avoiding fully showing up?" the horse insisted in a calm voice.

I closed my eyes and reflected on the areas of my life where I had been holding back. I thought about the projects I had started but never finished, the dreams I had pushed aside because I wasn't sure if I could succeed. I thought about the relationships where I had been present but not fully engaged, always holding a part of myself back out of fear of vulnerability.

"I've been holding back in many areas," I admitted, my voice quiet. "I've been afraid to fully commit because I didn't want to fail. But I see now that by not committing, I've been blocking the flow of prosperity into my life."

The horse's eyes gleamed with approval, and it took a step closer, its presence both grounding and empowering. "When you commit fully," it said, "you align yourself with the flow of abundance. Life rewards those who show up—those who are present, who engage fully, and who move forward with determination. Prosperity flows to those who are committed to their path."

The horse's words filled me with a sense of resolve. I could see now that by showing up fully—by being present and engaged in every area of my life—I could invite more prosperity, more opportunities, and more joy into my world.

"How does committing fully to your goals and dreams allow prosperity to flow more easily?" the horse asked, its voice filled with quiet strength.

I thought about it. When I committed fully, I would no longer be holding back. I would be giving my energy, my focus, and my time to the things that mattered most. And in doing so, I would be opening the door to new opportunities, new connections, and new sources of abundance. By showing up fully, I would be signaling to the universe that I was ready to receive, ready to create, and ready to succeed.

"It allows prosperity to flow because I'm no longer blocking it with hesitation or fear," I said, my voice stronger now. "When I commit fully, I'm fully aligned with my goals, and that alignment invites abundance."

The horse nodded, its eyes gleaming with approval. "Exactly. Prosperity flows where there is commitment, where there is presence. When you show up fully, you invite abundance to meet you on your path."

The horse stepped forward, its powerful body radiating strength and determination. "Begin by reflecting on the areas in your life where you are not fully present or committed," it said. "Write them down, and ask yourself how showing up fully in these areas can open new doors to prosperity."

I nodded, already thinking of the areas where I needed to show up more fully—my work, my relationships, my personal growth. I could see how committing to these areas, giving them my full attention and energy, would lead to new opportunities and a greater sense of fulfillment.

"And this week," the horse continued, "pick one area where you can increase your commitment. Take action on it. Whether it's a project you've been putting off, a relationship that needs more of your presence, or a personal goal you've been neglecting—show up fully for it. You'll see how that commitment invites prosperity into your life."

I smiled, feeling a surge of excitement. I was ready to commit, ready to show up fully for my life. The horse's wisdom had given me the strength to move forward with confidence, knowing that my commitment would be met with abundance.

The horse turned and began to move again, its powerful body flowing effortlessly through the open field. The hare, always by my side, nudged me gently, as if to remind me that this was a journey I could embrace with strength and confidence.

"Remember," the horse said, its voice fading as it galloped into the distance, "prosperity flows to those who show up fully. Commit to your path, and abundance will follow."

I stood tall, feeling the strength of the horse within me. I whispered the affirmation aloud with belief

Affirmation:
"I show up fully for life, knowing that abundance flows when I am present."

Growth Work for Home Play:

Full Presence:
Write down five areas in your life where you feel you are not fully present or committed. Reflect on how showing up fully in these areas can open up new opportunities for prosperity. How would committing fully to these areas change your life?

Commitment Challenge:
Do you avoid social gatherings too Often? Hide from being Clicked by Camera or do not show up on video calls? Do you also don't talk about yourself and your work for the fear of being judged or that you may bve Boring?
This week, pick one area where you can increase your commitment, whether it's in your personal life, career, or a relationship. Take action to show up fully in this area, and notice how your commitment invites new opportunities and prosperity into your life.

Discussion Points:

1. Where in your life are you holding back or avoiding fully showing up?
2. How does committing fully to your goals and dreams allow prosperity to flow more easily?

As I returned from my journey, I felt a deep sense of strength and determination. The horse had shown me that by showing up fully—by committing to my path with purpose and focus—I could invite more prosperity and abundance into my life. With each step I took, I knew I was moving forward with confidence, ready to embrace the opportunities that awaited me.

Hare whispered in my Dreams; For Expanding Your Willingness to Receive, the ideal spirit animal guide would be the Deer. The deer represents gentleness, sensitivity, and receptivity. It symbolizes the ability to receive with grace and openness, embracing vulnerability without fear. The deer teaches us to allow abundance into our lives by being open and willing to receive from others and from the universe.

The deer will guide you to expand your willingness to receive by helping you soften your barriers, trust the flow of life, and gracefully accept the abundance that is offered to you. It encourages you to be open, gentle with yourself, and ready to receive all forms of prosperity.

Chapter 16

The Deer's Grace – Expanding Your Willingness to Receive

The day was peaceful, a soft breeze moving through the leaves of my oak tree as I sat down for another journey. Today, I was feeling contemplative, thinking about the times in my life when I had struggled to receive. Whether it was help, love, or even material abundance, there were moments when I felt uncomfortable or unworthy of the gifts that life was offering me. But now, I was ready to change that. I was ready to learn how to expand my willingness to receive and to allow the flow of abundance to enter my life without fear, guilt, or hesitation.

Closing my eyes, I felt the familiar mist of my shamanic journey surround me, soft and cool. The hare was with me, as it always was, guiding me through the unknown. But today, I needed a different kind of guide—one that could show me how to receive with gentleness, grace, and trust. I needed a spirit animal that embodied receptivity, openness, and quiet strength.

As the mist cleared, I found myself standing in a tranquil forest. The trees were tall and ancient, their branches stretching out like welcoming arms. The sunlight filtered softly through the canopy, casting dappled light on the forest floor. I breathed in the fresh scent of pine and earth, feeling a sense of calm wash over me. In the distance, I caught a glimpse of movement—something delicate and graceful, moving silently through the trees. It was a deer.

The deer's presence was gentle yet powerful, its movements so fluid and quiet that it seemed to float over the forest floor. Its large, dark eyes were filled with wisdom and peace, and I could feel its energy—soft, receptive, and completely open to the world around it. The hare stood by my side, watching quietly as the deer stepped closer, its presence calming and soothing.

The deer approached me with a sense of quiet confidence, its eyes meeting mine with a gaze that seemed to see straight into my heart. There was no fear, no hesitation—only grace and openness. This creature knew how to receive, how to move through the world with trust and gentleness, and I knew that it was here to teach me how to do the same.

"You seek to expand your willingness to receive," the deer said, its voice soft and melodic, like the rustling of leaves in the wind. "But you have been holding back, haven't you?"

I nodded, feeling a wave of recognition wash over me. The deer's words were true. There had been so many times in my life when I had resisted receiving—whether it was a compliment, a gift, or even an opportunity. I had always felt like I had to prove myself worthy before I could accept anything, and that belief had held me back from truly allowing abundance to flow into my life.

"Yes," I said quietly. "I've struggled with receiving. I've always felt like I needed to earn it, like I wasn't worthy unless I had done something to deserve it."

The deer's eyes softened, and it took a gentle step closer. "You are not alone in that," it said, its voice filled with understanding. "Many people feel unworthy of receiving, but that belief is what limits their ability to experience true abundance. The universe is always offering, always giving, but you must be willing to receive with an open heart."

The deer's words resonated deeply within me. I could feel the truth of what it was saying—that my own self-doubt, my own fear of being unworthy, had created barriers to receiving. I had closed myself off from the flow of abundance because I didn't believe I deserved it.

"Where have you limited your ability to receive abundance in the past?" the deer asked, its eyes watching me closely.

I thought about the times when I had rejected help because I didn't want to appear weak, the times I had brushed off compliments because I didn't believe they were true, the times I had felt guilty for receiving anything that I hadn't worked hard to earn. All of those moments had been driven by a deep-rooted belief that I wasn't enough—that I wasn't worthy of receiving unless I had proven myself first.

"I've limited myself in so many ways," I admitted, my voice barely a whisper. "I've felt unworthy of receiving, like I had to earn everything before I could accept it."

The deer nodded, its gaze filled with compassion. "That belief has held you back, but it does not need to anymore. Receiving is not about proving your worth—it is about opening yourself to the gifts that are already flowing to you. The more you are willing to receive, the more abundance will flow into your life."

I felt a wave of relief wash over me as the deer's words sank in. I didn't need to earn everything. I didn't need to prove myself worthy before I could receive. I simply needed to open myself to the flow of life, to trust that abundance was already available to me, and to allow it in.

"How can you expand your willingness to receive in all areas of life?" the deer asked, its voice soft and encouraging.

I closed my eyes and thought about it. I could start by letting go of the belief that I had to earn everything. I could begin to trust that I was already worthy of receiving, simply because I was alive, because I was part of the flow of the universe. I could practice receiving with gratitude, without guilt or hesitation. And I could remind myself that receiving was not selfish—it was a natural part of life.

"I can expand my willingness to receive by letting go of the belief that I need to earn everything," I said, my voice growing stronger. "I can open myself to receiving with gratitude, without guilt or fear."

The deer's eyes gleamed with approval, and it stepped even closer, its presence gentle yet powerful. "Exactly," it said softly. "Begin by reflecting on the times when you felt uncomfortable or unworthy of receiving. What beliefs were at play? How can you change them?"

I nodded, already thinking of the times when I had resisted receiving because I didn't feel deserving. I could see now that those beliefs were not true—they were simply stories I had been telling myself. And now, it was time to change those stories.

"And for the next week," the deer continued, "practice saying 'thank you' every time you receive something, no matter how small. Whether it's a compliment, a kind gesture, or an opportunity, receive it with gratitude. This will help you open up to receiving more."

I smiled, feeling a sense of peace settle over me. The deer's wisdom was exactly what I needed. I could feel the barriers I had built around receiving beginning to soften, and I was ready to allow more abundance into my life.

The deer, sensing that its message had been received, took a graceful step back, its movements quiet and fluid. The hare, always by my side, looked up at me, its eyes filled with quiet support.

"You are worthy of receiving," the hare said gently. "The universe is always offering—allow yourself to accept its gifts."

I whispered the affirmation aloud, letting it settle into my heart:

Affirmation:
"I receive what I am willing to allow into my life."

Growth Work for Home Play:

Receiving Reflection:
Reflect on any times where you felt uncomfortable or unworthy of receiving abundance. What beliefs were at play, and how can you change them? Write about how you can shift your mindset to allow more abundance into your life.

Receiving Exercise:
For the next week, practice saying "thank you" every time you receive something, no matter how small. Whether it's a compliment, a gift, or an opportunity, receive it with gratitude and notice how this simple practice opens you up to more.

Discussion Points:

1. Where have you limited your ability to receive abundance in the past?
2. How can you expand your willingness to receive in all areas of life?

As I returned from my journey, I felt a deep sense of peace and openness. The deer had shown me that receiving was not something I needed to earn—it was something I could allow, with grace and gratitude. With each step I took, I knew I was opening myself more fully to the abundance that life had to offer, ready to receive with an open heart and a willing spirit.

Hare whispered in my Dreams; For Shifting from Scarcity to Abundance, the ideal spirit animal guide would be the Squirrel. The squirrel is associated with preparation, resourcefulness, and abundance. It symbolizes the ability to gather and store resources for the future, while also trusting that there will always be enough. The squirrel teaches us to shift our mindset from scarcity to abundance by recognizing that there are always opportunities and resources available if we are open to them.

The squirrel will guide you to let go of scarcity thinking, embrace resourcefulness, and trust in the flow of abundance in your life. It encourages you to gather and use what is available, while maintaining a positive and abundant mindset.

Chapter 17

The Squirrel's Wisdom – Shifting from Scarcity to Abundance

The crisp air of early autumn filled my lungs as I sat beneath my familiar oak tree. The leaves were just beginning to turn gold, hinting at the changing seasons. Today, I was feeling a deep need for transformation—specifically, in how I viewed money and abundance. For as long as I could remember, I had operated from a place of scarcity, always worried that there wasn't enough, that I needed to save and hold on tight just in case. But I knew that this mindset was holding me back from truly experiencing prosperity. Today, I was ready to shift from scarcity to abundance.

With a deep breath, I closed my eyes and began my shamanic journey. As always, the hare was with me, guiding me through the swirling mists. But today, I knew I needed a spirit animal that embodied resourcefulness, abundance, and the ability to gather and trust. I needed a guide that could show me how to shift my mindset and embrace the idea that there is always more than enough.

As the mist cleared, I found myself standing in a sun-dappled forest, the ground beneath my feet soft with fallen leaves. The scent of pine and earth filled the air, and I could hear the quiet rustling of animals in the underbrush. In the distance, I saw a small but quick figure darting between the trees, its movements fast and purposeful. It was a squirrel.

The squirrel moved with agility and confidence, scurrying up trees and across branches with ease. It carried a small acorn in its mouth, stopping occasionally to dig into the soft earth and bury its treasure. The hare, ever present, watched quietly as the squirrel made its way toward me, its eyes bright with purpose.

As the squirrel approached, I felt a sense of calm and clarity. This small creature, so often seen as simple and playful, carried a deep wisdom about abundance. It knew how to gather and prepare, but it also trusted in the cycles of nature. The squirrel didn't operate from fear—it operated from a place of resourcefulness, knowing that there was always enough to gather, store, and share.

"You've come to shift your mindset from scarcity to abundance," the squirrel said, its voice light but wise, like the rustling of leaves in the wind. "But you've been holding on too tightly, haven't you?"

I nodded, feeling the weight of the squirrel's words. For so long, I had believed that saving money was the only way to protect myself from the uncertainty of the future. I had lived with the constant fear that there wouldn't be enough—that if I didn't hold on tightly to what I had, I would lose everything. But standing here in the presence of the squirrel, I realized how limiting that belief had been.

"Yes," I admitted quietly. "I've been saving out of fear, not from a place of trust. I've always worried that there wouldn't be enough."

The squirrel tilted its head, its eyes sparkling with understanding. "That is the mindset of scarcity," it said gently. "When you believe there isn't enough, you close yourself off from the flow of abundance. But when you trust that there is always more than enough, you open yourself to receiving and creating prosperity in all forms."

The squirrel's words resonated deeply with me. I could feel the truth in what it was saying. By holding on so tightly—by saving out of fear—I had been operating from a mindset of lack. I had been telling myself that there wasn't enough, and that belief had shaped my entire relationship with money. But now, I was ready to change that. I was ready to trust in the flow of life, to believe that abundance was always available to me.

"How have scarcity beliefs shaped your financial habits?" the squirrel asked, its voice soft but insistent.

I thought about it. My saving habits had always been driven by fear—fear of not having enough, fear of losing what I had, fear of the unknown. I had spent so much time worrying about the future that I hadn't allowed myself to fully enjoy the present. I had saved not out of a desire to grow and create, but out of a deep-rooted belief that I needed to protect myself from inevitable loss.

"I've been saving out of fear," I said softly. "I've been holding on so tightly because I didn't believe there was enough to go around."

The squirrel nodded, its eyes filled with compassion. "And how would that change if you shifted to a mindset of abundance?" it asked gently.

I closed my eyes and imagined it—what my life would look like if I believed that there was always more than enough. I could see myself saving money not out of fear, but out of a desire to grow my resources. I could see myself investing in experiences that brought me joy, sharing my abundance with others, and trusting that there was always more to come. The weight of scarcity lifted from my shoulders, and I felt a sense of lightness and freedom.

"It would change everything," I whispered, a smile forming on my lips. "I would feel free. I would trust that there is always more than enough."

The squirrel smiled, its small paws clutching an acorn. "Exactly," it said, its voice filled with quiet wisdom. "When you trust in the flow of abundance, you open yourself to receiving more. Prosperity is not about holding on tightly—it's about gathering, sharing, and trusting that the universe always provides."

The squirrel took a step closer, its movements quick and purposeful. "Begin by reflecting on your current saving habits," it said. "Are they driven by fear, or by the desire to grow and create? Write down how you can shift from scarcity to abundance, and commit to one action that reinforces your belief in abundance."

I nodded, already thinking of the ways I could begin shifting my mindset. I could start by saving from a place of trust—by believing that I was growing my resources, not protecting myself from loss. I could also practice generosity, giving freely to others and trusting that what I gave would return to me tenfold.

"And this week," the squirrel continued, "take one action that reinforces your belief in abundance. Whether it's giving a small amount of money to someone in need or investing in something that brings you joy, You don't get rich by making More, But what you do with what you got. let this action remind you that there is always more than enough and you can choose to create more from it."

I smiled, feeling a deep sense of gratitude for the squirrel's wisdom. I was ready to let go of the scarcity mindset that had held me back for so long. I was ready to embrace abundance and trust in the flow of life.

The squirrel, sensing that its message had been received, darted back into the trees, its movements light and playful. The hare, always by my side, looked up at me, its eyes filled with quiet support.

"You are always provided for," the hare said gently. "There is always enough—more than enough. Trust in that, and you will see how abundance flows to you."

I whispered the affirmation aloud, letting it settle into my heart:

Affirmation:
"I shift from scarcity to abundance, knowing I have more than enough."

Growth Work for Home Play:

Scarcity to Abundance:
Reflect on your current saving habits. Are they driven by fear of not having enough, or by the desire to grow your resources? Write down how you can shift from a scarcity mindset to one of abundance and trust.

Abundance Action:
This week, commit to one action that reinforces your belief in abundance. Whether it's giving a small amount of money to someone in need, investing in something that brings you joy, or sharing your resources with others, let this action serve as a reminder that there is always more than enough.

Discussion Points:

1. How have scarcity beliefs shaped your financial habits?
2. How can shifting to an abundance mindset transform your relationship with money and savings?

As I returned from my journey, I felt a deep sense of trust and peace. The squirrel had shown me that abundance was always available to me, that there was no need to hold on so tightly or operate from fear. With each step I took, I knew I was moving toward a life of greater prosperity, ready to receive and share all that the universe had to offer.

Hare whispered in my Dreams; For Surrounding Yourself with Prosperity Influences, the ideal spirit animal guide would be the Elephant. Elephants symbolize strength, wisdom, loyalty, and community. They thrive in supportive, close-knit groups and are known for their strong bonds and ability to lead with wisdom. The elephant teaches us the importance of surrounding ourselves with positive influences and building a supportive network that nurtures our growth and prosperity.

The elephant will guide you to recognize the power of the company you keep, encouraging you to seek out relationships and environments that uplift, support, and inspire you toward prosperity.

Chapter 18

The Elephant's Wisdom – Surrounding Yourself with Prosperity Influences

The soft hum of the forest surrounded me as I sat beneath my oak tree, reflecting on the company I kept in my life. The familiar feeling of knowing that the people around me played a crucial role in shaping my mindset had been growing in my heart. I had begun to notice how the energy, conversations, and actions of those closest to me were influencing my own thoughts and behavior, especially around money and success. Some lifted me up, while others seemed to drain my energy. Today, I was ready to shift that dynamic and learn how to surround myself with prosperity influences—those who inspired, uplifted, and supported my journey toward abundance.

As I closed my eyes and allowed the mist of my shamanic journey to envelop me, the hare appeared beside me once again. Its gentle presence was familiar and comforting, but today, I sought a guide who embodied strength, wisdom, and the ability to lead with grace in the presence of a supportive community. I needed a guide who could show me how to build strong, prosperous relationships that would help me flourish.

The mist cleared, and I found myself standing in the heart of a dense jungle. The air was thick with the scent of earth and greenery, and in the distance, I could hear the soft, rhythmic rumble of a herd moving through the trees. As I looked around, I saw a massive figure emerge from the jungle—a magnificent elephant.

The elephant moved with quiet strength and dignity, its large body swaying gracefully as it approached. Its eyes, deep and wise, held a quiet knowing, as if it had seen the cycles of life play out over countless years. The hare remained close by, watching as the elephant stood before me, its presence both grounding and empowering.

"You seek to surround yourself with those who uplift and inspire you," the elephant said, its voice deep and steady, like the rumble of distant thunder. "But you've allowed some to drain your energy, haven't you?"

I nodded, feeling the weight of the elephant's words. It was true. I had spent too much time with people who didn't share my vision for prosperity—people who were stuck in scarcity thinking, negativity, or self-doubt. Their energy had weighed me down, making it harder for me to stay focused on my goals. But standing here in the presence of the elephant, I could feel the power of community and support. The elephant lived in a close-knit herd, surrounded by others who protected and uplifted one another. This was the wisdom I needed to learn.

"Yes," I admitted softly. "I've been spending time with people who drain me, people who don't believe in abundance. It's been affecting my mindset."

The elephant nodded, its eyes filled with understanding. "The people around you greatly influence your energy and your thoughts," it said, its voice resonating with calm authority. "When you surround yourself with those who uplift you, who believe in abundance, their energy flows into you, and you begin to thrive. But when you allow negative influences into your circle, they drain your energy and keep you stuck in scarcity."

I could feel the truth of the elephant's words settle deep within me. The people I spent the most time with had a direct impact on my mindset—whether I was focused on abundance or stuck in scarcity. If I wanted to truly embrace prosperity, I needed to surround myself with people who inspired me, who believed in abundance, and who encouraged me to grow.

"Who are the five people you spend the most time with?" the elephant asked, its voice gentle but insistent.

I closed my eyes and thought about it. I pictured the faces of those closest to me—friends, colleagues, family members. Some of them were supportive and uplifting, always encouraging me to pursue my dreams and believe in the possibilities of life. But others were more critical, more focused on limitations than on opportunities. I realized that while I valued these relationships, some of them were holding me back from fully stepping into my prosperity.

"I've been spending time with people who don't always uplift me," I admitted, my voice quiet. "Some of them drain my energy. But others inspire me—they believe in abundance, and their energy makes me feel more positive and hopeful."

The elephant's eyes softened, and it took a slow step forward, its massive body moving with grace. "Surrounding yourself with people who uplift and inspire you is essential to prosperity," it said. "When you are in the presence of abundant thinkers, their energy amplifies your own, and you begin to attract more of what you desire. But when you are surrounded by those who focus on lack, their energy pulls you down, making it harder for you to create the prosperity you seek."

I nodded, understanding now how important it was to be intentional about the company I kept. The people I spent the most time with had the power to either support my journey toward abundance or hinder it. And it was up to me to choose who I allowed into my circle.

"How can surrounding yourself with positive, abundant thinkers impact your prosperity?" the elephant asked, its deep voice resonating in the stillness of the jungle.

I thought about it. When I was around people who believed in abundance, I felt more confident, more motivated, and more open to opportunities. Their positive energy rubbed off on me, and I found myself thinking bigger, dreaming bigger, and taking bolder steps toward my goals. But when I was around those who doubted themselves or focused on scarcity, I felt weighed down, as if their energy was holding me back.

"It would change everything," I said quietly. "When I'm around people who believe in abundance, I feel more inspired, more hopeful. I start to believe that anything is possible."

The elephant nodded, its eyes filled with quiet approval. "Exactly. Your circle of influence is powerful. When you surround yourself with those who uplift and inspire you, you begin to reflect their energy. Prosperity flows more easily when you are in the presence of those who believe in it."

The elephant stepped closer, its presence calm and grounding. "Begin by evaluating your circle," it said gently. "List the five people you spend the most time with. Reflect on how they influence your mindset about money, success, and abundance. Do they uplift you or drain your energy? Are they positive, abundant thinkers, or do they focus on limitations and scarcity?"

I nodded, already thinking of the people I spent my time with and how their energy influenced my own. I could see now that it was time to be more mindful about who I allowed into my inner circle. It wasn't about cutting people out of my life—it was about making sure that the people I spent the most time with were those who supported my journey toward prosperity.

"And this week," the elephant continued, "make a plan to expand your circle. Reach out to new, inspiring people who share your vision of prosperity. Surround yourself with those who believe in abundance, and watch how their energy helps you grow."

I smiled, feeling a deep sense of gratitude for the elephant's wisdom. I was ready to evaluate my circle and make sure that I was surrounding myself with the kind of people who uplifted and inspired me. The elephant's gentle but powerful presence reminded me that I was not alone on this journey—and that the people I chose to surround myself with could make all the difference in my path toward abundance.

As the elephant turned and began to walk away, its massive body disappearing into the jungle, the hare nuzzled my side gently. Its quiet presence was a reminder that I was always supported, always guided on this journey.

"You are worthy of a circle that uplifts you," the hare said softly. "Surround yourself with those who inspire you, and watch how your life begins to flourish."

I whispered the affirmation aloud, letting it settle deep within my heart:

Affirmation:
"I am surrounded by people who uplift and inspire me to greater abundance."

Growth Work for Home Play:

Evaluate Your Circle:

List the five people you spend the most time with. Rate them on a scale of 1-10 (10 being Highest and 1 being lowest) on prosperity mindset they have. ***Complete this before you read further.***

Reflect on how they influence your mindset about money, success, and abundance. Do they uplift and inspire you, or do they drain your energy? Consider how you can spend more time with people who share your vision of prosperity.

Expand Your Circle:

This week, make a plan to reach out to new, inspiring people who align with your values and vision for prosperity. Whether through networking, mentorship, or friendships, commit to surrounding yourself with positive, abundant thinkers.

Discussion Points:

1. Who are the five people you spend the most time with? Do they uplift or drain your energy?
2. How can surrounding yourself with positive, abundant thinkers impact your prosperity?

As I returned from my journey, I felt a renewed sense of clarity and purpose. The elephant had shown me that my circle of influence mattered—that the people I chose to surround myself with could either help me grow or hold me back. With each step I took, I knew I was moving toward a life of greater abundance, ready to build a community that supported, uplifted, and inspired me on my path to prosperity.

Hare whispered in my Dreams; For Making Empowered Financial Decisions, the ideal spirit animal guide would be the Falcon. The falcon represents focus, clarity, and decisive action. Known for its keen vision and ability to strike with precision, the falcon symbolizes the power of making clear, intentional choices. It teaches us how to make empowered decisions by focusing on what truly matters and taking action with confidence and purpose.

The falcon will guide you in sharpening your focus, helping you make thoughtful, empowered financial decisions that align with your goals and values. It encourages clarity of vision and decisive action when it comes to managing your resources and prosperity.

Chapter 19

The Falcon's Vision – Making Empowered Financial Decisions

I sat under the shade of my oak tree, the rustling leaves above me mirroring the quiet thoughts swirling in my mind. Lately, I had been reflecting on the financial decisions I had made throughout my life. Some were impulsive, some were rooted in fear, and others in scarcity. But today, I wanted to learn how to make empowered, intentional financial decisions—ones that aligned with my highest good and allowed prosperity to flow freely.

Closing my eyes, I began my shamanic journey once more, the mists swirling around me as I traveled through the familiar landscape of my inner world. The hare, my steadfast guide, hopped alongside me. But today, I knew I needed a spirit animal who could teach me about precision, clarity, and decisive action. I needed a guide that could show me how to sharpen my focus and make empowered choices about money.

As the mist began to clear, I found myself standing on a rocky cliff, the vast sky stretching endlessly above me. The air was crisp and cool, and I could feel the powerful energy of the wind swirling around me. High above, a majestic figure soared, its wings slicing through the air with grace and precision. It was a falcon.

The falcon flew with a sense of purpose and clarity, its keen eyes focused on the world below. I watched in awe as it circled effortlessly in the sky, scanning the landscape with sharp focus before diving swiftly toward its target.

As the falcon landed gracefully on a nearby rock, its piercing eyes met mine, and I felt a surge of power and clarity wash over me. This creature, with its keen vision and decisive action, embodied everything I sought to learn about making empowered financial decisions.

"You seek to learn how to make empowered choices with your money," the falcon said, its voice sharp and direct, like the wind cutting through the air. "But you've been allowing fear and doubt to cloud your decisions, haven't you?"

I nodded, feeling the weight of the falcon's words. It was true. For so long, many of my financial decisions had been driven by fear—fear of not having enough, fear of making mistakes, fear of the unknown. I had acted from a place of scarcity, rather than abundance, and as a result, I hadn't always made the best choices.

"Yes," I admitted quietly. "I've been making decisions out of fear, and it's been holding me back."

The falcon's eyes narrowed, its gaze intense but filled with understanding. "When you make decisions from a place of fear, you limit yourself," it said, its voice strong and steady. "But when you make empowered decisions—decisions based on trust, clarity, and alignment with your highest good—you open the door to prosperity. It's time to sharpen your focus and choose wisely."

The falcon's words hit me like a bolt of lightning. I could see now that my fear had clouded my judgment, causing me to make financial decisions that weren't in alignment with my true desires. But standing here in the presence of the falcon, I felt a renewed sense of clarity and purpose.

"How do you currently make financial decisions?" the falcon asked, its voice cutting through the air like a blade.

I thought about it. Many of my decisions were reactive, based on fear or anxiety. When money felt scarce, I would make choices from a place of lack, trying to hold on tightly to what I had rather than trusting in the flow of abundance. I realized that I had been operating from a scarcity mindset, constantly worried about losing what little I had, instead of focusing on growth and prosperity.

"I've been making decisions based on fear," I said softly. "I've been holding on too tightly, afraid of losing what I have instead of trusting in abundance."

The falcon nodded, its eyes gleaming with understanding. "That is the mindset of scarcity," it said. "But you have the power to shift that. By making empowered financial decisions—decisions based on clarity, trust, and alignment with your highest good—you invite prosperity to flow freely into your life."

The falcon spread its wings slightly, as if to emphasize the freedom that comes with making empowered choices. "Begin by reflecting on the financial decisions you've made in the past," it said. "Were they based on scarcity or abundance? Write down ten decisions you've made about money, and reflect on how each decision shaped your financial reality."

I nodded, already thinking of the decisions I had made—some good, some not so good. I could see how fear had influenced many of them, and how a lack of clarity had caused me to make choices that weren't always in my best interest. But now, with the falcon's guidance, I was ready to change that.

"How can making empowered decisions lead to more prosperity?" the falcon asked, its voice filled with purpose.

I closed my eyes and imagined what it would feel like to make decisions from a place of empowerment. I saw myself weighing my options carefully, trusting in my ability to choose wisely, and making decisions that aligned with my highest good. I could feel the shift in energy—the confidence, the clarity, the sense of freedom that came with making empowered choices. I realized that when I made decisions from a place of abundance, I opened myself up to receive more.

"When I make empowered decisions, I trust in the flow of abundance," I said, my voice stronger now. "I align with what is best for me, and that invites prosperity into my life."

The falcon's eyes gleamed with approval, and it took a step closer, its presence powerful yet grounding. "Exactly," it said, its voice filled with quiet strength. "Your financial reality is shaped by the decisions you make. When you make empowered choices, you invite prosperity to flow freely. Practice making one empowered financial decision this week—something that aligns with your highest good, something that reflects trust in abundance rather than fear."

I smiled, feeling a surge of determination. I was ready to take control of my financial reality, to make empowered decisions that would lead me toward prosperity. With the falcon's sharp focus and the hare's quiet support, I knew I had the guidance I needed.

The falcon spread its wings, preparing to take flight once more. Its gaze met mine one last time, and I felt its wisdom settle deep within me.

"Remember," the falcon said as it lifted off into the sky, "prosperity flows when you make empowered decisions. Trust your vision, sharpen your focus, and choose with clarity."

As the falcon soared into the heavens, the hare nudged my side gently, its eyes filled with quiet encouragement.

"You have the power to make empowered choices," the hare said softly. "Trust yourself, and watch as prosperity unfolds."

I whispered the affirmation aloud, letting it settle deep within my heart:

Affirmation:
"I make empowered decisions with money that align with my highest good."

Growth Work for Home Play:

Exploration & Visualisation:

Write down 10 choices you may make about money. reach out to people who prosperity consciousness and ask for Advice. You must make these decisions based on Abundance and not from fear or Scarity Consciousness. Invite the energy of how these choices may look like and what can they create different in shaping your financial reality.

Empowered Choices:

Pick one from the above choices this week, Make that one empowered financial decision that aligns with your highest good. Whether it's investing in something that brings you joy or letting go of a financial fear, make your choice from a place of clarity and trust in abundance.

Discussion Points:

1. How do you currently make financial decisions? Are they based on fear or trust in abundance?
2. How can making empowered decisions lead to more prosperity?

As I returned from my journey, I felt a deep sense of clarity and focus. The falcon had shown me the power of making empowered decisions—decisions that were aligned with my highest good and driven by trust, not fear. With each step I took, I knew I was moving closer to a life of greater prosperity, ready to make choices that reflected my true vision for the future.

Hare whispered in my Dreams; For Releasing Rejection and Embracing Abundance, the ideal spirit animal guide would be the Butterfly. The butterfly symbolizes transformation, acceptance, and embracing change. It represents the beauty that comes from releasing old limitations and stepping into a new reality filled with abundance. The butterfly teaches us to let go of rejection, embrace growth, and allow abundance to flow freely, just as it transitions gracefully from a caterpillar to a butterfly.

The butterfly will guide you in releasing old patterns of rejection and fear, encouraging you to transform and fully embrace the abundance that life has to offer. Its journey from one form to another reflects the transformation you must undergo to fully receive abundance.

Chapter 20

The Butterfly's Transformation – Releasing Rejection and Embracing Abundance

The air was still and calm as I sat under my oak tree, the leaves whispering in the breeze. My mind, however, was not as quiet. I had been thinking about all the times in my life when I had said "no" to opportunities—whether it was a job offer, a financial opportunity, or even a small gift from a friend. Each time I rejected those moments, a part of me felt afraid or unworthy of receiving them. But today, I was ready to change that. I was ready to stop rejecting abundance and learn how to say "yes" to prosperity with an open heart.

As I closed my eyes and began my shamanic journey, the familiar mist surrounded me, swirling softly around my body. The hare appeared by my side, as it always did, a gentle guide through the unknown. But today, I needed a spirit animal that could show me how to transform—how to let go of the old patterns of rejection and step into a new reality where I could fully embrace abundance. I needed a guide that embodied growth, acceptance, and the beauty of transformation.

As the mist began to lift, I found myself standing in a meadow filled with wildflowers. The air was sweet with the scent of blossoms, and the soft hum of insects filled the space around me. As I looked up, I saw a delicate figure fluttering in the air—a butterfly.

The butterfly danced lightly on the breeze, its wings shimmering in the sunlight as it moved from flower to flower. There was an elegance to its movements, a grace that spoke of transformation and renewal. I watched as it fluttered closer to me, its bright wings a symbol of change and growth. The hare stood beside me, watching quietly as the butterfly landed gently on a nearby flower.

"You've come to learn how to release rejection and embrace abundance," the butterfly said, its voice soft and melodic, like the rustling of petals in the wind. "But you've been holding onto fear, haven't you?"

I nodded, feeling the truth of the butterfly's words settle deep within me. For so long, I had been rejecting opportunities—whether it was out of fear, self-doubt, or discomfort. I had turned away from moments that could have brought abundance into my life because I didn't believe I was worthy of receiving them. But standing here in the presence of the butterfly, I realized that it was time to change. Just as the butterfly transforms from a caterpillar into something beautiful and free, I, too, was ready to transform my relationship with abundance.

"Yes," I admitted softly. "I've been rejecting opportunities because I've been afraid—afraid of failing, afraid of not being good enough."

The butterfly's wings fluttered gently as it perched on the flower, its eyes filled with understanding. "Rejection is often born from fear," it said kindly. "When we reject opportunities or money because of fear or judgment, we block the flow of abundance. But just as I transformed into something new, so can you. By saying 'yes' to prosperity, you open yourself to all the gifts that life has to offer."

The butterfly's words resonated deeply within me. I could feel the truth of what it was saying—that my habit of rejecting opportunities had been limiting me, keeping me stuck in old patterns of scarcity. But I was ready to change. I was ready to let go of the fear and open myself to the flow of abundance, just as the butterfly opens its wings and embraces the beauty of the world.

"How often have you rejected opportunities because of fear or self-doubt?" the butterfly asked, its voice filled with gentle curiosity.

I thought about it. There had been so many times when I had turned away from opportunities because I didn't feel ready, because I didn't believe I was worthy, or because I was simply afraid of stepping out of my comfort zone. Each time I had said "no," I had unknowingly blocked the flow of abundance into my life.

"I've rejected so many opportunities because I was afraid," I said quietly. "I didn't believe I was worthy of receiving them."

The butterfly fluttered closer, its wings shimmering in the sunlight. "But you are worthy," it said softly. "And the more you say 'yes' to opportunities, the more abundance will flow into your life. When you embrace the opportunities that come your way, you open the door to prosperity in all its forms."

The butterfly's words filled me with a sense of hope and possibility. I could see now that every time I said "no," I was rejecting not just the opportunity, but the abundance that was waiting to come into my life. But now, I was ready to say "yes." I was ready to embrace the opportunities that came my way, to trust that I was worthy of receiving all the prosperity the universe had to offer.

"How can saying 'yes' to opportunities allow abundance to flow into your life?" the butterfly asked, its voice filled with quiet wisdom.

I closed my eyes and imagined what it would feel like to say "yes" to the opportunities that came my way. I saw myself opening up to new experiences, accepting the gifts that life offered, and trusting that each "yes" would lead me closer to the prosperity I desired. I could feel the shift in energy—the lightness, the freedom that came with releasing rejection and embracing abundance.

"When I say 'yes,' I allow abundance to flow into my life," I said, my voice growing stronger. "I open myself to all the possibilities that life has to offer."

The butterfly's wings fluttered softly in approval, and it hovered closer to me, its presence light and joyful. "Exactly," it said gently. "Begin by reflecting on the times you have rejected opportunities or money because of fear. Write down ten instances where you've said 'no,' and reflect on how you can say 'yes' to future opportunities."

I nodded, already thinking of the times when I had turned away from abundance because I was afraid. I could see now how those moments had been driven by fear and how they had blocked the flow of prosperity in my life. But with the butterfly's guidance, I was ready to change that. I was ready to transform, to embrace opportunities with an open heart, and to say "yes" to prosperity.

"And this week," the butterfly continued, "practice saying 'yes' to any opportunities or offers that align with your goals. Whether it's a small gesture of kindness or a financial opportunity, say 'yes' and watch how abundance begins to flow into your life."

I smiled, feeling a sense of lightness and freedom. The butterfly had shown me that I didn't need to be afraid of receiving. Just as the butterfly had transformed into something beautiful and free, I, too, was ready to transform my relationship with abundance. I was ready to release rejection and embrace all the prosperity that life had to offer.

As the butterfly fluttered away, its wings shimmering in the sunlight, the hare nuzzled my side gently, its quiet presence a reminder that I was always supported on this journey.

"You are worthy of receiving abundance," the hare said softly. "Say 'yes' to the opportunities that come your way, and watch how prosperity unfolds."

I whispered the affirmation aloud, letting it settle deep within my heart:

Affirmation:
"I no longer reject money or opportunities; I am open to all forms of prosperity."

Growth Work for Home Play

Rejection Reflection:

Write down ten instances where you have recently rejected money or opportunities because of fear or discomfort. Reflect on how you can say "yes" to future opportunities. Consider how releasing rejection can allow more abundance to flow into your life.

Openness Practice:

For the next week, practice saying “yes” to any opportunities or offers that align with your goals, no matter how small. Allow yourself to receive with an open heart and notice how abundance begins to flow.

Discussion Points:

How often have you rejected opportunities because of fear or self-doubt?

How can saying "yes" to opportunities allow abundance to flow into your life?

As I returned from my journey, I felt a deep sense of peace and freedom. The butterfly had shown me that rejection was simply a barrier I had placed in my own path, and that by saying "yes" to opportunities, I could invite abundance into my life. With each step I took, I knew I was moving closer to a life of greater prosperity, ready to embrace all the opportunities and abundance that awaited me.

Hare whispered in my Dreams; For Gratitude and Magic in Prosperity would be a wonderful idea! The unicorn symbolizes purity, magic, and infinite possibilities. It embodies the idea that magic exists in everyday life if we remain open to it. Unicorns are often associated with wonder, the unknown, and the mystical, making them perfect for a chapter focused on the magic that gratitude can bring into prosperity.

By speaking to a unicorn, you can emphasize the idea that gratitude is a key to unlocking the magical flow of abundance in life, helping you to see the beauty and potential in everything around you. The unicorn's mystical qualities make it an inspiring guide for appreciating the unseen forces that bring prosperity when we live in gratitude.

Chapter 21

Gratitude and Magic in Prosperity

As I entered the final phase of my shamanic journey, I found myself in a meadow bathed in golden sunlight. The soft breeze carried the scent of blooming flowers, and the atmosphere shimmered with quiet magic. I sensed my spirit animal guide, the Hare, nearby, but another presence was emerging—a creature of pure light and wonder.

The air around me swirled gently, and from the mist, a magnificent Unicorn appeared. Its mane sparkled like stardust, and its eyes radiated warmth and wisdom. I was in awe. The Unicorn trotted toward me gracefully, as if gliding through the very essence of the meadow. Beside it, the Hare watched calmly, offering a sense of grounded serenity amidst the surreal beauty of the scene.

"Welcome," the Unicorn's voice echoed softly in my mind, "Today, we speak of gratitude and magic—two forces that, when embraced, invite limitless prosperity."

I nodded, feeling both curiosity and a sense of deep peace. The Unicorn stood tall and luminous, while the Hare sat by, reminding me of the balance between wonder and practicality.

"Gratitude," began the Unicorn, "is the key to unlocking abundance. When you appreciate what you already have, you open the door to receive even more. Magic follows gratitude. It may seem impossible, but when you live in the flow of appreciation, things beyond logic happen effortlessly."

The Unicorn's words sank into me like sunlight warming my skin. I thought about my life—the moments where my gratitude had drawn in unexpected opportunities, where things beyond my wildest imagination had unfolded simply because I had opened my heart to possibility.

"How does gratitude influence your prosperity?" the Unicorn asked, tilting its head slightly, eyes glowing with curiosity.

I thought deeply. "When I focus on what I'm grateful for, everything seems to flow more smoothly. I stop worrying about what I don't have and start seeing the wealth already present in my life. It's as if by appreciating my blessings, I signal the universe to send more."

The Unicorn nodded. "Exactly. Gratitude is the language of abundance. And magic—true magic—emerges when you allow gratitude to permeate your being."

"Magic defies logic," added the Hare, ever wise. "It's when you surrender to the flow of life and let go of the need to control that the impossible becomes possible."

I recalled times in my life when things had unfolded in ways I couldn't have planned. One instance stood out—a job opportunity that appeared out of nowhere just when I needed it, or a chance meeting that led to a friendship that changed my life. These were moments of magic, woven with threads of gratitude.

The Unicorn, sensing my thoughts, smiled. "That's it. Magic lives in those moments. By embracing gratitude, you invite more of them."

The Unicorn leaned closer, its mane shimmering as it shared a simple yet powerful exercise.

"Each day," it said, "write down five things you are grateful for. Not just the material—like money or success—but also the things that can't be measured. Write about the love in your life, your health, your joy. Reflect on how each thing has contributed to your prosperity."

I nodded. "And what about magic?"

The Unicorn's eyes sparkled. "Think of a time when something magical happened, when life surprised you in the most beautiful way. Write about it. Reflect on how you couldn't have planned it, how it unfolded naturally. Remember that feeling, and live in that openness. The more you appreciate magic, the more it will show up."

Because...**Magic Lies at the End of Logic**

Standing between the wise Hare and the luminous Unicorn, I closed my eyes and repeated the affirmation they both guided me toward:

"I express gratitude for all that I have, and it multiplies effortlessly."

I felt a shift inside me—a sense of peace, possibility, and joy to Embody Prosperity in Every Area of Life

The Unicorn's soft voice echoed again. "You've completed this journey, but prosperity is a path you walk every day. It's not a destination—it's a way of being."

The Hare added, "By using the tools, affirmations, and Growth Work for Home Play you've learned, you'll continue to expand your prosperity. Trust that abundance flows to you naturally, through gratitude, magic, and the openness you've cultivated."

I reflected on the journey I had taken, realizing how much had shifted. I had learned that prosperity wasn't just about money—it was about living in the flow of abundance in every aspect of life.

Final Growth Work for Home Play

As the journey neared its end, the Unicorn offered me one final challenge:

Daily Gratitude Practice

Write down five things you are grateful for each day. Reflect on how each thing has contributed to your prosperity. Allow the energy of gratitude to multiply your abundance.

Magic Reflection

Recall a time when something wonderful and unexpected happened in your life. Write about this experience, reflecting on the magic that unfolded. How can you invite more magic into your life by living in gratitude?

Final Affirmation

The Unicorn and Hare stood together as I spoke the final affirmation:

"I embody prosperity in all areas of my life and invite abundance to flow effortlessly."

The meadow sparkled as if the very air was alive with the energy of possibility. I knew then that prosperity was not something to chase, but something to allow—to welcome into my life with open arms, guided by gratitude, magic, and my own spirit's journey.

Final Reflection

I turned to the Unicorn and the Hare. "What new possibilities am I ready to create now?" I asked myself.

Both the Hare and Unicorn gazed at me with knowing smiles, and I realized the answer had always been within me—waiting to be unlocked by the magic of gratitude.

Conclusion: Embodying Prosperity in Every Area of Life

As you complete this 21-chapter journey, you are equipped with the knowledge, tools, and mindset to create lasting prosperity in all areas of your life. Prosperity is not a destination but a way of being, and it requires consistent focus, gratitude, openness, and alignment with abundance. Each chapter has offered you opportunities to expand your awareness, make empowered choices, release limitations, and shift into a mindset of receiving. The Growth Work for Home Play, affirmations, and discussion points provided are designed to be revisited whenever you feel the need to realign with prosperity. Remember, prosperity is your birthright, and by embodying these principles, you are allowing abundance to flow freely into every aspect of your life—financial, emotional, physical, and spiritual.

Life is not about what you don't have; It is about what you do with what you have - Geet Batra

Final Affirmation:
"I embody prosperity in all areas of my life and invite abundance to flow effortlessly."

Ongoing Practice:

1. **Continue to use the daily affirmations and Growth Work for Home Play provided in this book.**
2. **Reflect on your growth regularly and stay open to new possibilities for expansion.**
3. **Trust in the flow of abundance and express gratitude daily for everything that comes your way.**

Final Discussion Point:

1. **What was your Biggest Takeaway?**
2. **What has shifted in your mindset and life since you started this journey toward prosperity with this Book?**
3. **What new possibilities are you ready to create now?**

Quotable Quotes FROM THE BOOK

"Life is not about what you don't have, it is about what you do with what you have"

******

"Magic lies at the end of logic"

******

"Magic needs to be embraced as it is, Why kill it with your logic"

******

"Freedom of choice is your Biggest Power; Do not sell it for Approval. "

******

"It takes more energy to hold on to resistance"

******

"Drop all significance, Do not tire yourself, Nothing means Nothing"

******

"Whatever you focus on grows"

******

"Future depends how present are you Now"

******

"Prosperity is not something you chase; it's something you allow."

******

"Focus on abundance, and you invite it into every corner of your life."

******

"Your choices create your reality—prosperity begins when you choose to receive it."

******

"Money is energy—treat it with joy, and it will flow effortlessly to you." "Judgments about money are barriers; release them, and prosperity will find you."

******

“Follow the inner light to light your world outside”

******

“Be you, Because only that makes you BE-YOU-tiful”

******

"True wealth isn’t about numbers in your bank account—it’s about richness in your heart, mind, and soul."

******

"Gratitude is the gateway to magic—what you appreciate multiplies."

******

"When you embrace your uniqueness, you open the door to unlimited abundance."

******

"You don’t need permission to receive abundance—allow yourself to be worthy now."

******

"The more you try to control money, the more elusive it becomes. Let go, and let it flow."

******

"Opportunity often knocks quietly—be still enough to hear it."

******

"Every 'no' to an opportunity is a 'no' to prosperity. Learn to say yes with courage."

******

"What you resist, persists. Release your fear of change, and watch prosperity unfold."

******

"You don't need to be 'good' to receive abundance; you only need to be open."

******

"True prosperity lies in the willingness to receive—not in how much you work or give."

******

"Each connection is a Bridge you may cross some day."

******

"In Oneness; there is no fear; Only in separation you would be alone."

******

"Joy doesn't require reason; happiness does!"

******

"If it doesn't work in the first place; try something else, Create more and then more; let's go."

******

"Nobody will be confident of you; unless you do."

******

"The purpose of life is to dream & play"

******

"If you play for Winning and not losing; its not playing anymore; have fun in whatever you do."

******

"No one can be you as much as you can; that's your abundance"

******

"Their judgement is their problem, not yours."

******

"They will never apologize for the choices they imposed on youYou might regret though"

******

"Money isn't the goal; it's the tool for creating a joyful, abundant life."

******

"Your value is not measured by your income but by the impact you make with your presence."

******

"When you show up fully for life, life shows up fully for you."

******

"Scarcity is a mindset, not a reality. Choose abundance, and the universe will reflect it back to you."

******

"In every moment of gratitude, you create space for miracles to enter."

******

"Prosperity is not about striving; it's about aligning with the flow of life."

******

"When you let go of fear, you make space for abundance to enter."

******

"Success is not measured by how hard you work, but by how fully you receive."

******

"Your spirit is your greatest asset; nurture it, and prosperity will follow."

******

“Get up, Dress up, Show up; there is no shortcut to showing up.” ****** “Receiving is Easy, refusing is the problem.

******

“There are No limitations, except the ones that you impose upon yourself.”

******

“Abundance is Believing that you can have more.”

******

“Be what you wish to have and keep acting relentlessly on what you be.” ******

“The past has no choice; Let go of it.”

******

“Perfection is not Beautiful; your tattered wings are.”

******

“Gratitude always Multiples”

******

"You are not chasing money, you are inviting it."

******

"The universe is abundant by nature—your job is to align with that abundance."

******

"Every step toward prosperity begins with a single belief: 'I am worthy of more.'"

******

"Release the need for control, and abundance will surprise you in ways you never expected."

******

"Money is neither good nor bad—it's a reflection of your relationship with yourself."

******

"The magic of prosperity begins when you stop seeking approval and start embracing who you are."

******

"The more gratitude you express, the more reasons life gives you to be thankful."

******

"Abundance isn't something that happens to you—it's something you create from within."

******

"In prosperity, there's no need for perfection—only the willingness to receive."

******

"True wealth comes when you stop looking outside and start cultivating abundance within."

******

"You don't need to do more; you need to receive more."

******

"The path to prosperity is paved with trust, not struggle."

******

"When you embrace change, you open the door to limitless possibilities."

******

"You are the sculptor of your reality—shape it with the energy of abundance."

******

"Money responds to how you treat it—treat it as a friend, and it will come to you often."

******

"Prosperity isn't just a destination—it's the way you choose to live each day."

******

Appendix: Prosperity Tools and Resources

Prosperity Tools and Resources

This appendix includes additional tools, techniques, and resources to help you maintain and deepen your journey toward prosperity.

Recommended Reading: Books and resources that align with the principles of abundance, wealth consciousness, and self-growth.

- 21 Days to Unlock the Power of Affirmations by Louise hay
- Walking With Wolf by Nithya Chellam
- Walking With Wolves by Nithya Chellam
- Animal Spirit Guides by Steven Farmer
- Power Animals by Lori Morrison
- Prosperity Consciousness by Chutisa & Steven Bowman
- How to Become Money Workbook by Gary M. Douglas
- How to Become Money Advanced Workbook by Gary M. Douglas

Hold the Space for my Upcoming Books on finding your Givation; Givation is your creation in Life to give to others from your Abundance, because when you share your abundance with others, you will receive abundance, While not necessarily from them; But the Universe has your back and will ensure that you get it.

What we give out, we get back - Louise L. Hay

Follow me on Social media for programs and workshops on Self-Discovery, Self-acceptance, Self-love and embracing your abundance.

Wishing you Magic, Love & Light

🪄💕✨✨✨✨✨

Geet Batra

ABOUT THE AUTHOR

Geet Batra is a Certified Life Coach from Grow More Avenues, ICF & Marshall Goldsmith Stakeholder-Centred Executive Coach, A Heal Your Life workshop Leader and a personal growth mentor. With almost 2 decades of experience in the corporate world; he set out on a Journey of helping individuals break through their limitations and expand into their full potential, Geet's facilitation focuses on creating a life of joy, ease, and abundance. Through workshops, seminars, and personal coaching, Geet has helped thousands of people shift their financial reality

and embrace prosperity in all forms.

Feel free to Explore my Social media presence

Website www.magicpossibilities.com

Youtube https://www.youtube.com/@magicpossibilities/

Instagram https://www.instagram.com/coachgeet/

Linkedin https://www.linkedin.com/in/coachgeet/

Soundcloud https://soundcloud.com/geetbatra

Email Coach@geetbatra.com

This detailed content gives you a complete guide to prosperity, integrating lessons,

practical Growth Work for Home Play, affirmations, and reflection points that allow you to embody

abundance effortlessly. Whether you are just starting your prosperity journey or

looking to deepen your practice, this book serves as a powerful companion on your

path to living a life filled with health, wealth, love, and joy.

www.ingramcontent.com/pod-product-compliance
Lightning Source LLC
Chambersburg PA
CBHW042126180726
48282CB00072BA/1264
* 9 7 8 9 3 3 4 1 4 3 8 4 3 *